THE LIVING WORD COMMENTARY

Editor
Everett Ferguson

The Letter of James

The Letter of James

J. W. Roberts

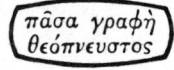

SWEET PUBLISHING COMPANY

Austin, Texas

© 1977 by Sweet Publishing Company.
All rights reserved. No part of this book may be reproduced by any means without permission in writing from the publisher, except for brief quotations embodied in critical articles, or reviews.

LIBRARY OF CONGRESS CATALOG CARD NUMBER: 76-51637

STANDARD BOOK NUMBER: 8344-0072-3

PRINTED IN U.S.A.

Acknowledgment

This commentary is based on the text of the Revised Standard Version of the Bible, copyrighted 1946, 1952, and 1971 by the Division of Christian Education, National Council of Churches, and used by permission.

Writers in *The Living Word Commentary* series have been given freedom to develop their own understanding of the biblical text. As long as a fair statement is given to alternative interpretations, each writer has been permitted to state his own conclusions. Beyond the general editorial policies, the editors have sought no artificial uniformity, and differences are allowed free expression. A writer is responsible for his contribution alone, and the views expressed are not necessarily the views of the editors or publisher.

Contents

I. INTRODUCTION ... 7
   A General Epistle ... 7
   Authorship ... 8
   Life of James ... 8
   Objections to James as the Author ... 12
   Relation to Other Books ... 20
   The Date of the Epistle ... 21
   The Form and Structure of James ... 22
   Outline of James ... 23
   Bibliography ... 25

II. THE LETTER OF JAMES ... 27
   Gifts of God Manifested in Trials, 1:1-18 ... 27
   Attitude toward the Word Which Begets, 1:19-27 ... 55
   The Sin of Respect of Persons, 2:1-13 ... 68
   The Relation of Faith and Works, 2:14-26 ... 82
   Notes on "Faith Alone" ... 98
   Admonition to Teachers, 3:1-18 ... 100
   Worldliness in the Church, 4:1-12 ... 121
   Direct Address to the Unbelieving Rich, 4:13–5:6 ... 138
   Attitude toward Mistreatment, 5:7-12 ... 151
   The Christian in Illness and Sin, 5:13-20 ... 161

EDITOR'S NOTE

J. W. Roberts wrote this commentary on James and privately published it in 1963. With the consent of his widow and children it is now being included in the Living Word Commentary. This step required modifications of the original book in three respects: (1) changing the text and comments from the American Standard Version to the Revised Standard Version, (2) conforming to the style of the present series, and (3) reducing the comments to fit the space requirements of the present series. For these adaptations the editor is responsible. An effort has been made to avoid substantive changes so that the commentary still says what the author originally said. Nevertheless, J. W. Roberts was always studying and not afraid to change his views. The insights found in some of the work on James listed in the revised bibliography done after his commentary was written would likely have gained his assent had he lived to produce a revised edition.

The dedication in the original edition read: "To Delno, my wife, who has been such a great help, not only on this, but on so many other undertakings." By changing "wife" to "friend" those words may stand as the words of the editor.

I

Introduction

A GENERAL EPISTLE

The epistle of James stands in the ancient arrangements of the New Testament under the "General (*katholikoi*) Epistles." This designation is used for the letters not considered as coming from Paul. The designation signifies that the letters were written to the church at large or a larger segment or section of the church. The term is fairly accurate for all except 3 John (possibly 2 John also), which is perhaps included because of the natural grouping of the three epistles bearing the name of John.

James is a good illustration of the way in which the term is employed. It is addressed "to the twelve tribes in the Dispersion." Whatever this difficult term means specifically, it indicates that the book was written to a large segment of the church, to scattered groups of Christians throughout the Mediterranean world, rather than to an individual Christian or to an individual church as were most of Paul's letters.

In some of the earlier manuscripts of the New Testament the General Epistles were placed immediately after the book of Acts. Jerome was the first to put them immediately after the book of Hebrews, where they have customarily been placed.

INTRODUCTION

AUTHORSHIP

The author of the epistle calls himself "James, servant of God and of the Lord Jesus Christ." There are four persons of this name in the New Testament: (1) James the son of Zebedee and brother of John, one of the three "innercircle" of the apostles of Jesus; (2) James the apostle, son of Alphaeus (Mark 3:18), the same as James the younger or less, the son of Clopas (Mark 15:40); (3) James the father (or brother) of Judas (not Iscariot) (Luke 6:16); and (4) James the brother of the Lord (Matt. 13:55; Gal. 1:19) and brother of Judas (Jude 1:1).

Of the four, the second and third are hardly to be considered, for they are known only by their names and do not figure greatly in the early history of the church. The James who wrote this epistle was so well known that he expected to be recognized by his title. James the brother of John, son of Zebedee, died a martyr's death under Herod Agrippa I before the year A.D. 44 (the year of Herod's death). The story is told in Acts 12:2. There have been a few scholars who thought that this James was the author of this epistle, but most students consider his early death to render this supposition unlikely. Thus it is most likely that the author is Jesus' brother according to the flesh. Objections to this view will be considered below.

LIFE OF JAMES

James stands first among the names of the four brothers and at least two sisters of Jesus in the family of Joseph and Mary (Matt. 13:54-56; Mark 6:3). Presumably he was the eldest, besides Jesus, followed by Joseph, Simon, and Judas.

The exact relationship of these children to Jesus has been the subject of much discussion. Theories concerning them held throughout the history of the church may be summarized with reference to James.

1. That he was a son of Mary and Joseph. This view was that of Helvidius (identity unknown), whose work claiming that Joseph was the father of James and his brethren by Mary was contested by Jerome. It is argued that this thesis may be

Identity of James

supposed from the relationship of Mary and Joseph and the implication of Matthew 1:24, 25 that Joseph knew her not until the birth of Jesus. Further it is argued that this is the natural conclusion from the description of these children as the brothers and sisters of Jesus. Tertullian argued from these facts that the sanctity of marriage is hallowed by the mother of Jesus living in wedlock and bearing children after the birth of Jesus, thus showing that some leaders of the church held this view (*On Monogamy* 8).

2. That he was a half brother of Jesus, a son of Joseph by a former marriage (the Epiphanian view, after Epiphanius, who did not invent the theory but who strongly argued the thesis in the latter half of the fourth century [*Heresies* LXXVIII]). The idea goes back to the apocryphal book of James (*Protevangelium*), which tells of the miraculous birth and early life of Mary (daughter of a couple known as Joachim and Anna). She was presented to the temple and brought up there. At the age of twelve she was betrothed (according to the story) to an aged widower Joseph, who was chosen by a sign from heaven.

There is no evidence for the theory except legend. Its real motivation was to supply a basis for the doctrine of the perpetual virginity of Mary. The argument is based on such inconclusive assumptions as that Jesus' own brethren would not have questioned his sanity; that he would not have left his mother with John if he had had brothers to take care of her; and that Joseph must have been much older than Mary because he seems to have vanished completely from the gospel story.

3. That he was a cousin of Jesus (the Hieronymian view, so called from Jerome, whose Greek name was Hieronymos). This belief, put forward in A.D. 383 and not previously documented, has become the stated opinion of the Roman Catholic church. Jerome's argument proceeds from the erroneous assumption that the word "apostle" used to describe James in Galatians 1:19 can only refer to one of the twelve apostles of Jesus. He reasons that he is thus to be identified with James the younger, the son of Alphaeus (since James the son of Zebedee is excluded). This James is also to be

INTRODUCTION

identified with one of the sons of Mary (James and Joses) at the cross (Mark 15:40 and compare Mark 6:3). Jerome then insists that the description "his mother's sister, Mary the wife of Clopas" in the list of the women at the cross (John 19:25 and compare Mark 15:40 and Matt. 27:56) refers to the same person. He thus concludes that the Mary of Mark 6:3 is not Jesus' mother, but her sister, the wife of Clopas, thus making Jesus and James cousins. He then assumes that this James is the same as James the younger and that his father was Alphaeus.

Against this contention it may not only be pointed out that Jerome began with an erroneous view of the word "apostle," which may be and is used in the New Testament in different ways from one of the twelve (as in Acts 14:14), but that James is repeatedly called Jesus' brother (*adelphos*). Too, the view rests upon the questionable interpretation of the passages listed above, especially that of John's list of women at the cross.

It may safely be concluded that James is an actual brother to Jesus in the flesh through the common mother, Mary.

Joseph the father of James is described as a "righteous," or "just," man (Matt. 1:19), which probably means that James was reared in strict observance of the law of Moses. It is interesting to note that all the children were named after illustrious Jewish ancestors. James was reared at Nazareth in Galilee, whence Joseph had returned after the trip to Egypt.

During the public ministry of Jesus, James as a part of the family viewed his messianic claims with the suspicion that he was beside himself (Mark 3:21) and sought to restrain him (Matt. 12:47; Luke 8:19). We are told that his brothers "did not believe in him" (John 7:5). At the cross, Jesus committed his mother to the beloved John rather than to the unbelieving brothers (John 19:26).

After the resurrection Christ appeared to James (1 Cor. 15:7) and this seems to have changed all, for immediately it is noted that he was among the number who waited during the interval before Pentecost (Acts 1:13, 14).

For the first few years of the church's history little is heard of James. But he gradually emerged as a figure of

Life of James

prominence in the Jerusalem church. Three years after Paul's conversion he returned to Jerusalem and visited James along with Peter (Gal. 1:18, 19). In the account of the visit 14 years later (Gal. 2:1ff.) James is referred to as one of the "pillars" of the church (Gal. 2:9). After the breakup of the apostolic band his name stands out, though the later tradition which pictures him as "the bishop of the church in Jerusalem" is a reading back into the New Testament of later developments (Eusebius, *Church History* II, i, 2-5).

James took part in the recognition of the Gentile mission of Paul (Gal. 2:9). The party which refused table fellowship with Gentiles claimed James' leadership—whether rightly we do not know (Gal. 2:12). At the meeting to decide the question of Gentile circumcision James sided with Paul and Peter and suggested the writing of a circular letter making known the decision (Acts 15:13ff.). He tempered the decision that the law is not enforced upon the Gentiles by suggesting that they defer to some of the deeply engrained ritual and morals of the Jews. Whether this is any more characteristic of James' concept of the gospel and its relationship to the Jews and the law than of Peter or Paul is not clear.

When Paul made his visit to Jerusalem bearing the gifts "remembering the poor" (Gal. 2:10; Acts 21:18ff.), James and the elders made the proposal to Paul that to counteract the influence of the zealous Jews Paul should become surety for the obligations of a group of poor worshipers who had taken a vow (Acts 21:20ff.).

James' attitude in these glimpses of him has been interpreted as typical of Palestinian or Judaistic Christianity. First, his Hebrew or Jewish background is taken as basic. But he is also seen in the dual role of championing the freedom of the Gentiles from the law (as Paul contended) while at the same time being zealous for the observance of traditional Judaism for Jewish Christians. This is probably to be interpreted as a measure of statesmanship aimed at winning his nation to the claims of the gospel. Some have questioned whether the arrangements for Paul's actions in Acts 21:20ff. existed because the full light of revelation had not yet been thrown on the relation of the law and the gospel as it was later

INTRODUCTION

in the books of Hebrews and Ephesians or whether they are to be explained merely as the prerogative of Jewish conscience (as in Rom. 14; 1 Cor. 8) which is permissible on social grounds (cf. 1 Cor. 9:20; Acts 16:3), a prerogative which exists only as a liberty and must not be insisted on for others or thought of as a part of righteousness under the gospel (Col. 2:16; Gal. 4:9, 10; 5:4; 2:4, 5). This question has important bearing upon the interpretation of the epistle of James, for it is often represented as exhibiting a type of Christianity not yet freed of its Jewish shackles, so that it is mainly interested in an orientation of the church to Judaism.

James' later life is revealed to us only from Josephus (*Antiquities* XX, ix, 200) and Hegesippus (Eusebius, *Church History* II, xxiii). Here he is seen as a man of great piety, commanding by reputation the respect of Jew and Christian alike and exercising great influence not only in Jerusalem among his nation and the church but also among Christians of the Dispersion who came to Jerusalem for the Jewish feasts. He is pictured as rigorous in his religious exercises, living the life of a Nazirite. His life ended in martyrdom at the hands of the enraged Jews, who threw him from the temple and stoned him to death in the year 62.

The role thus described by the Scriptures and tradition fits perfectly the letter of James as we have it. Often it is difficult to tell if Jews or Christians are addressed, and it may well be that he wrote to Christians of his nation but still with an eye to his countrymen to whom he hoped to appeal by virtue of his reputation and esteem for holiness. But in the absence of an apologetic note for the claims of Christ and the gospel this must not be pressed too far.

OBJECTIONS TO JAMES AS THE AUTHOR

The Arguments Considered

In modern times many critics have doubted that James the Lord's brother could be the author of the epistle of James. The arguments against the genuineness of James may be summarized under four points: (1) The Greek of the epistle is too good to have been written by an Aramaic-speaking Jew such as James. (2) The style of the epistle shows a familiarity with certain stylistic features of Greek literature which would be quite unlikely for James. (3) There is an absence of mention of Jesus and his teaching such as would be expected if written by a brother of the Lord. (4) James had a difficult time of gaining acceptance into the canon. Easton in the *Interpreter's Bible* argues that these objections are overwhelmingly against James writing the epistle, and he adopts the theory of Meyer that the book is a Jewish production written in imitation of Jacob's address to the twelve tribes in Genesis 49. He thinks that some Christian writer took over the book and added some Christian sections and put the book out as a Christian document. We will examine these ideas in detail.

The Greek Style. It is argued that the epistle furnishes us with one of the two or three best examples of Greek idiom in the New Testament (along with Hebrews and parts of Luke's writings). This is an acknowledged fact, though it needs some explaining. Considering that James the Lord's brother was a native of Galilee, where the native tongue would be Aramaic, it is thought impossible or at least most improbable that James could have written with the mastery of Greek that is exhibited in this epistle. Easton says,

> Could we by the wildest stretch of imagination, think of James in mature life as learning to write the Greek of this epistle—an epistle cast in the Hellenistic and non-Semitic form of prose paraenesis, using the equally Hellenistic and non-Semitic diatribe, characterized by familiarity with Stoic-Cynic ethical terminology, and the Greek hexameters in 1:17 and 4:5? Or that, as in 4:6, he would cite the Old Testament (Prov. 3:34) from the Greek version (LXX), which is quite unlike the Hebrew?

He concludes: "Our epistle was not written by James the Lord's brother nor by any other James known to us by name in the New Testament" (p. 6). This argument has some weight, but one wonders if it is not actually an example of critical dogmatism. If the life of James were known in detail

INTRODUCTION

and if it were known that James did, in fact, never learn to write Greek in this fashion and if there is no possibility of the book's being written by James and presented in its present shape in such a case, then there might be some reason for such a dogmatic and positive statement.

But the facts are against these conditions. Nothing is known of James' education, his language ability, or opportunity. Besides this epistle, no known writings from his pen exist by which one might point in contrast to his acknowledged style. It is well known, on the other hand, that there was a deep penetration of Greek influence into Palestine affecting Galilee especially. Bethsaida, for example, not far from Nazareth, was known for Greek as its native tongue. James perhaps spoke Greek from childhood. How polished he might have become over a long period of contact and communication with Greek-speaking Jews is a question no one can answer. Certainly, if, conscious of his leadership, he had studied to equip himself to communicate better, it is not unreasonable that he could have done so. It is noted in the account of his death by Hegesippus that visitors from afar (Jews and Gentiles) sought out his counsel. Another possibility is that James wrote in Aramaic and procured someone in the church who could write good Greek to translate the epistle for his audience. Such a theory has, in fact, been urged by Wordsworth and later revived by Burkitt.

There is another factor, however. In addition to writing excellent Greek, James is still influenced by the Hebrew-Septuagint language background which was a part of his training. Several constructions and expressions which have their meanings largely from the Septuagint background show that James did not write "pure Greek." They fit perfectly the assumptions either that the book was written by a Palestinian Jew who first spoke both the Aramaic and Greek and went on from this to become proficient in the Greek tongue, or that an original document was translated into Greek by one with such a background.

If it is asked whether a Palestinian Jewish leader would quote from the Septuagint instead of the Hebrew, one replies that the motive and audience would determine. It should be

Authorship

remembered that James wrote for a Hellenistic audience, the Jews scattered in the Dispersion. Such Jews did use the Septuagint. How natural, then, that James, even if his natural bent was to use the Hebrew (a conclusion of which we are completely ignorant), should use the Greek version in writing to them.

Use of Literary Devices. The charge that James copied the Stoic diatribe style and made use of other Greek literary devices not ordinarily at the command of a Palestinian Jew is overdrawn. As is pointed out in the comment on James 4:13-5:6, the direct address or apostrophe is more characteristic of the Old Testament prophet "burden" apostrophe than it is of the Greek diatribe. Metzger has shown that such style is common among the Jewish writings of the Talmud (*Interpreter's Bible,* "The Language of the New Testament," vol. 7, p. 51). The coincidence of a sentence or two with a rhyme scheme may be a conscious quotation learned from an acquaintance, but more likely (as in other New Testament instances) it is pure coincidence. The same points may be made with respect to Paul.

Lack of Mention of Jesus. This argument is stated by McNeile as follows:

> It is difficult to think that a brother of the Lord, who had become a believer in Him, writing certainly before A.D. 69—some think at a much earlier date—could have written without speaking of His death or resurrection (unless a veiled reference to His death is to be seen in v. 6), and have contented himself with naming Him only twice (i. 1; ii. 1)—or only once, if, as is probable, the name in the latter passage is an interpolation. Although he refers to words of our Lord (see below), he shows little sign, such as we see in 1 Peter, of His "personal spell."

Actually this same charge is made against the genuineness of Peter (see A. M. Hunter in the *Interpreter's Bible,* vol. 12, pp. 77ff., who answers the charge effectively). But the question raised does not take into consideration the nature of the epistle. James is not writing a theological or Christological

INTRODUCTION

treatise. Other critics have seen in the reticence to parade his relation to Jesus a sign of James' modesty and a note of genuineness. An impostor, anxious to claim the authority of James for his work, would hardly have touched so lightly on the family tie.

But this charge ignores one of the most significant things about the epistle, that of the detailed reflection of the actual words of Jesus, especially from the speeches of Jesus like the Sermon on the Mount. If James does not reveal the "personal spell" of Jesus, he does show a baptism into the thought and words of Jesus.

Ropes (pp. 38ff.) lists the following parallels: 1:8 = Matthew 7:7; Luke 11:9; 2:5 = Matthew 5:3; Luke 6:20; 3:18 = Matthew 5:9; 4:4 = Mark 8:38 (cf. Matt. 12:39; 16:4); 5:1-6 = Luke 6:24; 5:12 = Matthew 5:34-37. To this Ropes adds that it is much more significant that the epistle shows an inclination to follow some of the broad interests of the Gospels. He lists especially the emphasis on hearing as well as doing (Matt. 7:21-29; Luke 6:46; Matt. 7:24-27; Luke 6:47-49; Matt. 25:31-46); the value set on poverty, the warnings to the rich, with the injunctions to prayer and devotion to God (1:9; 5:1ff.; cf. Matt. 6:19-34); the restraint in judging and unkind speech (5:9 with Matt. 7:1ff.). To these details many more may be added such as mention of the length of the famine in Elijah's time (5:17 with Luke 4:25); the parable of waiting for the harvest (5:7ff. with Mark 4:26-29); "the judge is standing at the door" (5:9 with Matt. 24:33).

It is not that such ideas may not be found scattered throughout other literature; but it is difficult to explain, as Ropes says, "the special and strong interest in them found alike in the compilers of the Gospels (or of their source) and in James." Of course there are missing terms and ideas (like Son of man and kingdom of God), but one does not expect the whole vocabulary and gauntlet of thought of the Gospels in five short chapters. Such an astute critic as Mayor lists 59 resemblances between James and the Synoptic Gospels and stars 26 of these as being of "the most importance." To these he adds 39 from the Johannine literature (written later but sharing the common debt to the remembrance of the teaching

Canonicity

of Jesus), of which 16 are starred as of more importance. He concludes, "Close as the connexion of sentiment and even of language in many passages, it never amounts to actual quotation, but is like the reminiscence of thoughts often uttered by our Lord, and sinking into the heart of a hearer who reproduces them in his own manner" (*Commentary,* lxxxv-xci).

The Late Acceptance into the Canon. This objection is stated by McNeile as follows, "The lack of early evidence and the slowness with which the epistle was received as canonical are unfavorable to the idea that it was written by the head of the mother-Church of Christendom." While there is some truth to the claim that James was somewhat late in emerging as fully canonical in that process of the church's identification and collection of its books, the facts need to be spread out and looked at before they influence us to say that the church made a mistake in that process. James shared with Jude, Revelation, 2 Peter, and 3 John the fate of being not too well known and thus falling under suspended judgment until they could prove their claims. The early church defined its canon or list of scriptural books in the process of debate with the Gnostics, an early group of heretics. Marcion's acceptance of only a very limited cutting of the New Testament books led the church to examine its own thinking. Four tests of canonicity were important: (1) a writing should be apostolic; if not being written by an apostle, then it should be traceable back to a known companion or contemporary of the apostles so that its origin could be seen to lie in the first age of the church; (2) it must have been used universally, not having been known only by one segment of the church; (3) it must show itself worthy to be read in the churches; (4) it must prove that its contents were able to edify the churches.

James easily met all these tests except that of universality. Here it was known in the Greek Church, but less well in the Syrian and especially the Latin. Origen at the end of the second century was the first to expressly quote it as being from James (*On John,* xix). Eusebius put it among the disputed books (*Church History* III, xxv) and he says of it, "Such is the story of James, whose is said to be the first of the Epistles

INTRODUCTION

called Catholic. It is to be observed that its authenticity is denied, since few of the ancients quote it, as is also the case of the Epistle called Jude's, which is itself one of the seven called Catholic; nevertheless we know that these letters have been used publicly with the rest in most churches" (*ibid.* II, xxiii). Some Latin writers (e.g., Rufinus) often quoted it but as from "the apostle James" (*Hom.* viii, *On Exodus*). In this he may well have been influenced by Paul's language in Galatians 1:19, in referring to "none of the other apostles except James the Lord's brother." Though it is not quoted in the extant writings of Clement of Alexander, he is expressly said to have given concise explanations "of all the Canonical Scriptures" and to have included James (Eusebius, *Church History* VI, xiv). Its first appearance in a Latin manuscript is said (Barclay) to be in Codex Corbeiensis (c. 350). But its appearance in Jerome's Vulgate assured it a place in the Latin tradition for all time. The epistle was included in the Syriac version of about A.D. 412 (Peshitto) though 2 Peter, 2 and 3 John, and Revelation are omitted; but whether it goes back to the older tradition is not clear. Cyril of Jerusalem (*Catech.* 4. 5. 33) included it among the canonical books.

It is fair to admit that this evidence is not overwhelming in favor of James, but this fact must not be weighed wrongly. Clearly in the absence of an official apostolic list of scriptural books, some books would be less well known and have more trouble getting recognition. If James and some of the other books were to be discarded as nongenuine, there would then still exist other books less well known than the rest, and the process could be continued backward until the last. When this lack of specific attributing of the epistle to James is allowed to have so much weight, one cannot help feeling that James is suffering from the overskeptical attitude of its critics and from the general tendency of late-dating of the New Testament epistles.

Arguments for James' Writing

External Evidence in the Apostolic Fathers. Of far more significance to this writer is the fact that the language and thought of James are so interwoven into the fabric of the

Influence

earliest Christian writers that it seems clearly to have been a part of the reading and hearing of the church from the beginning. It is not so much that it is quoted directly as being from James but that again the evidence consists of reminiscences of James' words which have sunk into the hearts of the writers, who reproduce them in their own words.

Let us take a few examples. The epistle of 1 Clement (written around A.D. 96) says, "Abraham the friend was found faithful in his obedience" (10:1; cf. James 2:23); "Rahab the harlot was saved because of faith and hospitality" (1 Clement 12:1; cf. James 2:25); "let the wise show forth his wisdom not in words but in good works" (38; cf. James 3:13). The *Shepherd of Hermas* (*Visions* III. ix. 6) speaks of "those rejoicing in wealth" and then (like James 5:4) warns that "their groans go up to the ears of the Lord." Again in *Similitudes* I.8 he echoes the specific "visit the widows and fatherless" of James 1:27. He warns with James 1:8 that he who prays should "ask in faith not doubting, not doubleminded" (*Mandate* IX. 3-9). James 4:7 is reflected in "Resist the devil and having been conquered he will flee from you in shame" (*Mandate* XII. v. 2). James 4:12 is echoed in "fear him who is able to save and destroy" (*Mandate* XII. vi. 3).

The epistle of Polycarp (died A.D. 155) clearly conflates the qualifications of 1 Timothy 3:1ff. with the instructions of James to visit the sick and the widows and orphans (*Epistle to the Philippians* 6). Elders are to be compassionate converting the erring (cf. James 5:19), visiting all the sick (1:27; 5:14), not neglecting the widows and orphans, abstaining from all wrath, respect of persons (same word as James 2:1).

Irenaeus (*Against Heresies* IV. xvi. 2) joins the words "Abraham believed God and it was imputed to him for righteousness" with "and he was called the friend of God," just as James joins the passages from Genesis 15:6 and Isaiah 41:8; 2 Chronicles 20:7. It would be quite a coincidence that different writers should do this independently.

There is a natural explanation for the epistle's lack of early acceptance. James the Lord's brother, though referred to by Paul as one of the pillars of the church, was not an apostle. After the fall of Jerusalem and the break of the church with most of Judaism, the Jewish church would naturally cling to James, and this would have lessened the hold which his memory would have on the rest of the church. Moreover, the letter was directed to and had become the property of the Jewish churches of the Dispersion. Since these tended to hold aloof from the other churches, this created an obstacle to the epistle's becoming generally known. It is possible that the seeming contradiction of James with Paul's doctrine of justification by faith may have contributed.

Internal Evidence. There are other arguments which favor the view that James the Lord's brother was the author. (1) The fact that there is a Hebrew cast to the Greek of the epistle; (2) that it fits well into the background of the Jewish situation as known from Acts and Josephus; (3) that, if James had written a letter, it would probably be a general letter, just such as we have in this one (this is in consideration of his position as leader of the Jerusalem church); (4) that it represents Christianity largely in its early Jewish state, dealing mostly with moral and ethical problems, often with little which even an orthodox Jew might not himself stress, but reflecting in detail the early teaching of the Lord Jesus in such sections as the Sermon on the Mount; (5) that the thesis helps to understand the likelihood that Peter and Paul knew the work (see below); (6) that there are resemblances between the letter of James and the wording of the letter suggested by James in Acts 15 (two curious points: the greeting expressed by a Greek infinitive and the use of the words "name called upon you" from the Old Testament in James 2:7; Acts 15:17); (7) that there is no satisfactory alternative to the theory of James as the author.

RELATION TO OTHER BOOKS

James has a close affinity to many other books both of the New Testament and of Jewish apocryphal books. The question is discussed at length in Mayor's commentary. Mention has already been made of the parallel in the early church fathers as evidence of the early knowledge of the book by

Date

Christian writers. Too, it has been emphasized that James' thoughts are permeated with the very words as well as the thoughts of the Gospels. There are significant parallels between James, Galatians, and Romans. The similarities to 1 Peter are strong (cf., for example, the recurrence in both of the phrases "various trials" and the "testing of your faith" in James 1:2 and 1 Peter 1:6, 7).

James' language in the original often has many parallels to the Jewish Apocrypha, especially the books of Wisdom and Sirach. It should naturally be expected that such books from the heritage of the period between the Testaments would be familiar to a Jew such as James was. That James may have made use, either directly from the books or because they were "in the air" or speech of his environment, is not to be thought strange. The Holy Spirit certainly made use of the natural vocabulary and mode of expression of the different writers. That their styles differ is proof of this. It is often almost a commentary itself to check parallel uses of a Greek expression in other writers. This often helps us to understand what the writers mean. We have made some use of this material in the present work.

THE DATE OF THE EPISTLE

Josephus' and Hegesippus' accounts give us conflicting dates for the death of James. Josephus places it at the time of the death of Festus, which would be in A.D. 62. Hegesippus places it just before the beginning of the siege of Jerusalem by Vespasian, which would be about A.D. 68. It does not appear which of these is correct, though most are inclined to accept the earlier date. Our present epistle agrees in every respect with the conclusion that it was written before the events of the destruction of Jerusalem. The destruction of the temple provided the clean break of the Jews and the synagogue from Christianity, and it is most unlikely that the epistle with its implied address to the Jews at large would fit a later date. Assuming that James is the author, we come to a date in the early 60s or earlier.

INTRODUCTION

The picture given of James in our documents shows him coming to a position of leadership after the death of James the son of Zebedee (Acts 12, A.D. 44). This date then becomes the earlier terminus from which the letter could have been written. Before this time would also hardly give time for the scattering and location of the Jewish Christians in the Dispersion or of the building up of congregations among them (Acts 11:19ff.). A date much earlier would also not account for the persecutions mentioned in the book. It has frequently been argued that the letter must have been written before the meeting in Jerusalem (Acts 15), which is variously dated around 47-49, because the letter does not mention the controversy over Judaism (but see the comment on James 4:11). There is some weight to this, though it is an argument from silence. The height of the strife and wars of the Jews characterized by the jealousy and warring faction which finally led to the destruction of Jerusalem may possibly favor a late date, not too long before the death of James.

THE FORM AND STRUCTURE OF JAMES

The epistle consists largely of small sections, some of which themselves consist of a grouping together of "sayings" or "maxims." The relationship of the different sections (and of the parts within the sections) to each other is often only apparent and must be adduced by the reappearance of the key ideas or words which are introduced in one place and picked up and expanded later (cf. control of the tongue in 1:26 with the section 3:1ff.). James' favorite device for tying his sections together is repeating some idea or word brought in incidentally at the end of one paragraph and then made the subject of the next section (cf. the word "lacking" in 1:4, "lacking in nothing" with "If any of you lacks wisdom" of the next verse). This device, which is technically called *duadiplosis,* is perhaps the outstanding stylistic feature of the epistle (cf. "no doubting" and "for he who doubts" in 1:6).

This loose structuring of a document along practical and ethical lines without a dominant theme was common in Hebrew literature (especially in wisdom literature, that is, Proverbs, etc.). Its technical name is "gnomology" (from the

Greek word *gnomē,* meaning "proverb"). Parallels exist, too, in the practical sections of Paul's epistles (e.g., Rom. 12ff.; Col. 3:1-5:4), in the Letter to the Hebrews (especially ch. 13) and in the hortatory sections of 1 Peter. When the admonitions were given in the second person "you" (as in 2:20; 4:13; 5:1), the advice is sometimes called "paraenesis" (from the Greek *par-aiteō,* "I advise"). This style is familiar from the Old Testament prophetic apostrophe sections (where a writer turns aside to address an opponent in direct language) and in rabbinical literature. Thus the efforts to find the main parallel and motif for the epistle of James in the sermonic style of the Greek Stoic preacher (the diatribe) are probably misplaced.

OUTLINE OF JAMES

James is not a book which lends itself to detailed analytical treatment. It has often been asserted that James cannot be outlined but that only a listing of the subjects treated in succession may be drawn up. But the more this writer has studied James, the feeling has grown that there is more unity and cohesion than appear at first sight. The book opens with a consideration of the place of trials in the Christian's life. This subject is extended through the subtopics of wisdom, poverty and riches, and the relation of trials to temptation to do evil. The assertion that God may be responsible for temptation leads to a denial and an exposition of the good gifts which God does give, especially the gift of salvation, through the word of truth. This leads James into a discussion of the power of the word to save those who receive it in the right way. But James insists that the word must be a vital factor. It must be active in both positive and negative ways in our lives, in good deeds, and in morality. Then, beginning with chapter 2, James discusses a number of sins or attitudes, which are mostly enlargements of things previously mentioned. He discusses the relation of faith and partiality (2:1-13), faith and works (2:14-26), wrong use of the tongue (3:1-18), and worldliness or not keeping "oneself unstained from the world" (4:1-12). All these seem related to the theme of James 1:19-27. The remainder of the book picks up the thread of the difficulties and trials of Christians: 4:13-5:6

INTRODUCTION

is an apostrophe addressed to the rich persecutors of Christians; 5:7-12 teaches Christians their proper attitudes in the midst of persecutions, admonishing patience and forbidding to swear. The rest of the book continues the general treatment of attitudes in the midst of difficulties, especially sickness and sin. First, a general admonition to prayer in troubles is given (5:13), followed by instruction in illness to call for the elders of the church (5:14, 15). Where the contingency exists that the sick one may be a sinner, instruction is given as to how to deal with the sin (5:15b, 16). Prayer is held out as the solution to difficulty, and assurance is given that prayer will avail (5:17, 18). Finally, in view of the peril of the sinner, an exhortation encouraging the strong to rescue the erring closes the epistle (5:19, 20). Thus without manufacturing connections which do not exist, it is possible to see an overall unity of subject and design in the letter.

OUTLINE OF JAMES

I. GIFTS OF GOD MANIFESTED IN TRIALS, 1:1-18
  A. Salutation and Greeting, 1:1
  B. The Joy of Trials, 1:2-4
  C. Wisdom in Trials, 1:5-8
  D. The Trials of Poverty and Riches, 1:9-11
  E. Patient Endurance in Trials Rewarded, 1:12
  F. Temptations Negatively Considered: They Do Not Come from God, 1:13-16
  G. The True Nature of God's Giving, 1:17, 18

II. ATTITUDE TOWARD THE WORD WHICH BEGETS, 1:19-27
  A. Meekness in Hearing the Word, 1:19-21
  B. Being Doers of the Word as Well as Hearers, 1:22-25
  C. The Application: Pure and Vain Religion, 1:26, 27

III. THE SIN OF RESPECT OF PERSONS, 2:1-13
  A. Partiality in the Assembly, 2:1-4
  B. God's Judgments, 2:5-13

IV. THE RELATION OF FAITH AND WORKS, 2:14-26

Bibliography

V. ADMONITION TO TEACHERS, 3:1-18
   A. Bridling the Tongue, 3:1-12
   B. The Truly Wise Teacher, 3:13-18

VI. WORLDLINESS IN THE CHURCH, 4:1-12
   A. The Source of Wars and Strife, 4:1-10
   B. Judging Brethren, 4:11, 12

VII. DIRECT ADDRESS TO THE UNBELIEVING RICH, 4:13-5:6
   A. The Presumptuous Use of Time, 4:13-17
   B. The Sin of Shameful Wealth, 5:1-6

VIII. ATTITUDE TOWARD MISTREATMENT, 5:7-12
   A. Admonition to Patience, 5:7-11
   B. Swearing Forbidden, 5:12

IX. THE CHRISTIAN IN ILLNESS AND SIN, 5:13-20
   A. Prayer and Singing, 5:13
   B. Illness and the Efficacy of Prayer, 5:14-18
   C. Converting Erring Brethren, 5:19, 20

BIBLIOGRAPHY

Commentaries on the Greek Text

Carr, Arthur. *The General Epistle of James.* Cambridge Greek Testament for Schools and Colleges. Cambridge University Press, 1899.

Huther, J. E. *Critical and Exegetical Handbook to the General Epistles of James, Peter, John, and Jude.* New York: Funk & Wagnalls, 1887.

Mayor, J. B. *The Epistle of St. James.* London: Macmillan and Co., 1913.

Oesterley, W. E. *The General Epistle of James.* The Expositor's Greek Testament. Edited by Rev. W. Robertson Nicoll. London: Hodder and Stroughton, 1897-1910.

Ropes, James Hardy. *A Critical and Exegetical Commentary on the Epistle of St. James.* The International Critical Commentary. Edinburgh: T. & T. Clark, 1916.

INTRODUCTION

Wordsworth, Christopher. *The New Testament of Our Lord and Saviour Jesus Christ in the Original Greek*. Vol. 3. London: Rivingtons, 1863-1881.

Commentaries on the English Text

Barclay, William. *The Daily Study Bible*. 2nd ed. Edinburgh, Saint Andrew Press, 1955-1960.

Blackman, E. C. *The Epistle of James: Introduction and Commentary*. Naperville, Illinois: Allenson, 1957.

Dibelius, Martin. *James*. Revised by Heinrich Greevan. Hermeneia. Philadelphia: Fortress Press, 1976.

Easton, B. S. "The Epistle of James." *The Interpreter's Bible*. Vol. 12. New York: Abingdon Press, c1957.

Knowling, R. J. *The Epistle of St. James*. Westminster Commentaries. London: Methuen & Co., 1910.

Lenski, R. C. H. *The Interpretation of the Epistle to the Hebrews and of the Epistle of James*. Columbus, Ohio: Wartburg Press, 1946.

Randall, G. H. *The Epistle of James and Judaic Christianity*. Cambridge, 1927.

Robertson, A. T. *Studies in the Epistle of James*. Rev. and ed. by Heber F. Peacock. Nashville: Broadman Press, 1959.

Ross, Alexander. *The Epistles of James and John*. The New International Commentary on the New Testament. Grand Rapids: Eerdmans, 1954.

Tasker, R. V. G. *The General Epistle of James*. The Tyndale New Testament Commentaries. Grand Rapids: Eerdmans, 1957.

Special Studies

Burkitt, F. C. *Christian Beginnings*. London: University of London Press, 1924.

Farrar, F. W. *The Early Days of Christianity*. New York: John W. Lovell Company, 1882.

McNeile, A. H. *An Introduction to the Study of the New Testament*. 2nd ed. Revised by C. S. C. Williams. Oxford: Clarendon Press, 1953.

Ward, Roy. "The Communal Concern of the Epistle of James." ThD Thesis, Harvard, 1966.

II

The Letter of James

GIFTS OF GOD MANIFESTED IN TRIALS, 1:1-18

Salutation and Greeting, 1:1

[1] In the typical fashion of good Greek correspondence James has three main elements in the salutation: He names himself as the author, gives the "twelve tribes in the Dispersion" as the recipients of the letter, and includes the "greeting."

The English name **James** is derived from the Italian form *Giacomo*. The Greek is equivalent to our "Jacob" and is, in fact, the same word that is translated "Jacob." The name was fairly common in Palestine. In this study **James** is assumed to be James the brother of Jesus. He was not one of the twelve but rose to prominence in the church at Jerusalem after the stoning of Stephen. Compare Acts 12:17; 15:13; 21:18; 1 Corinthians 15:7; Galatians 1:19; 2:9, 12; Mark 6:3 and Matthew 13:55 (see the Introduction). We assume that James writes as a leader prominent in the church at Jerusalem. He has in mind the problems of the church scattered abroad. He probably was in contact with the churches through the continual travel to Jerusalem of those coming to the feasts and for other business. It is known from contemporary accounts that James was held in great reverence and esteem as a righteous man and a leader of the church.

JAMES 1:1 — *Servant of God*

> **[1] James, a servant of God and of the Lord Jesus Christ,**
> **To the twelve tribes in the Dispersion:**
> **Greeting.**

From the Old Testament point of view the term **servant** (Greek "slave") was a term of honor and carried a meaning close to that of "worshiper." It had been worn with honor by Jewish worthies: Abraham, Isaac, and Jacob (Deut. 9:27); Joshua and Caleb (Judges 2:8; Num. 14:24); Job (Job 1:8); Moses (1 Kings 8:53; Dan. 9:11); and Isaiah (Isa. 20:3). It was especially used of the prophets (Amos 3:7; Zech. 1:6; Jer. 7:25). It was used collectively of the church at Jerusalem in one of the early narratives (Acts 4:29). There is probably also a subtle blending of this Old Testament religious significance and the more common secular meaning of the word, which was that of a civil slave. The slave had no rights, privileges, or will of his own. He owed complete submission and loyalty to his master, who actually held the power of life and death over him. James' use from this background would, then, be a conscious term of humility, of self-denial, and of loyalty. It would carry the affirmation that the will of God and Christ is the only rule of faith and life for one belonging to the church.

Notice there is a complete lack of claim to special prestige or attention as a brother of Jesus. Some have thought this unnatural, but it is a mark of modesty. Paul usually joins some other title with his frequent use of the term "servant," such as "apostle" (Titus 1:1). Only in Philippians 1:1 and Jude 1:1 do we find the term used singly in address as here.

The use of the term **servant** for "slave" is said to be confined largely to early American usage and English biblical translations. The present custom is to keep the two words sharply separate; hence, perhaps "bondservant" would convey the meaning of the original.

The twelve tribes was a synonym for the nation of Israel as a whole (Acts 26:7). It is true that the twelve tribes no longer existed as settled units in Palestine. We speak of the "lost tribes of Israel," thinking of the ten tribes taken into Assyrian captivity (2 Kings 17). But many of the individual members of such tribes knew their tribal identity. Even so,

The Twelve Tribes — JAMES 1:1

the term was spiritualized to include the nation without regard to the loss of identity of the tribes.

There are different understandings of how James uses the term here. Some contend that the book was written originally to Jews—fleshly Israel as God's people. This would be the literal meaning of the expression. This is unlikely, however, in view of the book as it now stands. So it is assumed by some that the present book has been worked over by a Christian hand and that the references to Jesus and the distinctly Christian material have been added to the original, which was addressed to Jews only. Of this there is no evidence. It is unlikely that Christians would have so appropriated such a writing. Also it has been pointed out that it would have been unlikely that anyone would have attempted to reach such a widely separated group as all the scattered people of the Jews.

A second meaning is that **twelve tribes** is equal to "Israel," used figuratively for the church. In Luke 22:30 ("You shall sit on thrones judging the twelve tribes of Israel") Jesus seems to use "twelve tribes of Israel" in this way. This idea of the "Jew" as the spiritual worshiper of God under the gospel rather than a physical descendant of the fleshly offspring of Jacob is quite well documented. Paul said, "For we are the true circumcision, who worship God in spirit, and glory in Christ Jesus, and put no confidence in the flesh" (Phil. 3:3). Compare Romans 2:29 and 9:6. This may also be the meaning of "Israel" in Galatians 6:15. In Revelation 7:4ff. those sealed as the servants of God are presented as 144,000, out of "every tribe of the sons of Israel." Thus it is quite possible that James is simply using this figurative way of addressing the whole church of Christ.

There is, however, a third possibility. There are those who insist that the term "twelve tribes of Israel" as spiritualized in the above manner refers only to the remnant of faithful Jews who accepted the gospel and thus that it means all "Christian Jews." Though it does not seem possible, overall, in the New Testament to limit the term "Israel" in this way, there does seem much to support the idea that James is written especially to Jewish Christians. The book is Jewish to the core. There is little or nothing which would imply that the writer had a Gentile group in view. It is plausible to this writer that James the Lord's brother had in mind Jewish Christians as those whose interests were closest to him and that, though **the twelve tribes** may mean "the whole church," particular stress is laid on that part allied to his own concern—the Jewish part.

The KJV's "scattered abroad" is better translated by "diaspora" as a technical term for all Israel living outside of Palestine—the **Dispersion.** In New Testament times Israelites were living in "every nation under heaven" (Acts 2:5-11). This exile from their native land had taken place over a long period of time and in many ways. First, it had been the result of forced removal at the times of the captivities of the Northern Kingdom (to Assyria, 721 B.C.) and then of Judah (to Babylon, 606-586 B.C.). The people of Judah retained their identity by refusing to intermarry with their captors. The great monument of this residence in Babylon is the Babylonian Talmud, an immense library of commentary on the law. Josephus bears witness that many such Jews remained in the East to his day. Hillel, the grandfather of Gamaliel (Paul's teacher), had been educated in Babylon. Much later the Romans at the capture of Jerusalem (63 B.C.) carried many Jews into slavery, from which many of them were eventually freed to constitute the "Freedmen" class (Acts 6:9). But many Jews moved out of Palestine of their own accord. According to 2 Kings 25:26 Jews in large numbers removed themselves to Egypt out of fear of the armies of Nebuchadnezzar. Alexander the Great (d. 323 B.C.) enticed many Jews to different parts of the empire with offers of special privileges. More than a million Jews were said to reside in Alexandria, the capital of Egypt. Egypt even saw the building of a temple there for Jewish worshipers. In Syria, in Cyrene of North Africa, in Crete, and all over Asia Minor the Jews lived and set up their synagogues. At one time Antiochus the King of Syria transplanted two thousand families from Babylon to the provinces of Lydia and Phrygia. So widespread was this scattering that the first-century geographer Strabo said, "It is hard to find a spot in the whole world that is not occupied and dominated by Jews." This

Greeting JAMES 1:1

Dispersion is witnessed in the book of Acts as the reader sees Paul visiting the synagogues for his first contacts with the community.

The book of James, then, in all probability was written to Jewish Christians living among the **Dispersion**, with special thought given to those living in the regions nearer to Palestine where the book might reach.

The form of this **Greeting** is peculiar to this passage among the epistles of the New Testament. It occurs elsewhere in the New Testament in Acts 15:23 (the letter of the church at Jerusalem to their Gentile brethren suggested by James) and in Acts 23:26 (the letter of the tribune Claudius Lysias to Felix the Governor). In the original it is an infinitive used as an imperative. The verb literally means "to be happy" or "rejoice." But it was used as an informal greeting meaning something like our "Hello" or "How do you do." At the beginning of a letter, as here, it is simply a salutation, and the rendering **Greeting** is a good way of expressing it in English.

The form of salutation used by James is more formal than is usual in New Testament letters and presents evidence of a more stylistic language in this letter.

The Joy of Trials, 1:2-4

The first section of the epistle seems to include verses 2-18. The central idea is that God is the giver of every good and perfect gift (vs. 17). The benefits of God are, however, often paradoxical; they often seem to be burdens and difficulties instead of blessings. The case in point is the difficulty or trials to which Christians are often subjected. The right view of these trials is presented, with the implied suggestion that wisdom is needed from God to accept this conception of suffering. This wisdom is promised as an answer to believing prayer. In this connection a warning is given to the doubting petitioner. As such trials seem heaped upon the poor disciple, James presents a view of the acceptable attitude of both the poor and the rich. James then promises the reward for faithful endurance of temptations. He assures the readers that temptations cannot be thought of as

JAMES 1:2 — Joy

²Count it all joy, my brethren, when you meet various trials,

coming from God, as he gives only good gifts. Finally, the supreme gift of all—salvation (presented under the figure of birth into the family of God)—is mentioned. The material of this section is calculated to help us count our blessings even in the midst of seeming adversity.

The first subject treated, then, in the epistle is that of trials and the way they are to be received by Christians. The idea is not that trials are pleasant in themselves but that, since they are beneficial to the individual, they are to be received gladly rather than with sorrow and despair. Their main effect is to produce perfection in the Christian's character by developing steadfastness.

[2] The word **count** means to "reckon" or "consider." It is not to be thought that trials are to be courted because they are enjoyable. It is only when they are understood to be the occasion of benefit that they may be reckoned as **joy** and received as such. **All joy** probably means "every kind of joy." The **joy** is as varied as the manifold tests themselves. Others take the idea as that of "pure joy," "nothing but joy" (cf. Acts 4:29, "complete candor"). The sufferer is to be glad that he can suffer. He is not to dwell on the unpleasantness of the experience. There should be no such thing as a complaining, grumbling disciple of Jesus. We must develop the attitude of Jesus, who "for the joy that was set before him endured the cross" (Heb. 12:2).

Fifteen times in the course of the epistle James uses the expression **my brethren**. Both the Greek and Hebrew words for "brother" originally have reference to those born of the same mother or womb. The Hebrew developed the wider sense of relative (Gen. 13:8, where Abraham called his nephew Lot his brother). It was used of tribal relationship, of those who belonged to the same group or people (Ex. 2:11; Lev. 19:17). It could even apply to a covenant brother (Amos 1:9), or to a friend (as David and Jonathan, 2 Sam. 1:26). James uses it here in the wide sense of fraternal relation of those born together into the family of God. His frequent use

Trials JAMES 1:2, 3

³for you know that the testing of your faith produces steadfastness.

---

of the term is a touch of humility and affection, though he exhorts pointedly and strongly at times (James 2:1ff.).

The **trials** under consideration are outside the man. As the man in the story of the good Samaritan "fell among" the robbers, so the Christian in the course of this life will encounter (**meet**) many things from without which will test him within. Usually such experiences will catch him unawares. He cannot anticipate what they will be or just when they will come. He cannot be prepared for the circumstance of each; he can only be prepared in attitude for whatever form it may take.

The word **trials** may have the sense of "temptation" (enticement to sin), but this does not fit the context. David prayed that God would try or test his heart and mind (Ps. 26:2). The meaning "trial of suffering" is well known to Jewish literature (*Sirach* 6:7; 27:5, 7). In Revelation 2:2 the sense of "trying or testing" of false teachers (by examining their teaching) is found. In verse 13 James uses the word in the sense of enticement to sin, but he is warning against taking his former use (in the passage now being discussed) as meaning that. It is most certain that James here has the sense of "testings" or "trials" in mind.

Various means that the writer has no specific kind of trials in mind but thinks that there are many possible ways of being tested. James later mentions the oppression by the rich (2:6), being dragged to court and having the honorable name blasphemed (2:6, 7), the keeping back of wages due one (5:1ff.), and even the killing of the righteous (5:6). Then of course there is the passage on sickness (5:13ff.). See also Hebrews 10:32ff.; Romans 5:3; 8:18ff.; 1 Thessalonians 2:14f.

[3] The Hebrew idea of "knowledge" tends toward the idea that knowing is an act of the will, i.e., an acknowledgment. One must himself allow something to be said to him. Compare such passages as 1 Samuel 2:12; Isaiah 1:3; Jeremiah 2:8; 9:2-5; Psalms 9:10; 36:10; Daniel 11:32. This does not mean to learn or make sure of something, but to recognize and accept the consequence of something which is revealed to one. Hence the verb is used often to call special attention to something, by way of warning. See Matthew 24:43; Luke 10:11; Ephesians 5:5; 2 Timothy 3:1; 2 Peter 1:20; 3:5.

The reason the Christian is to count or reckon an unpleasant trial as a joy is that he is to **know** or recognize from his instruction as a Christian that there is value to him in the experience. That regard comes when the testing of faith works **steadfastness**. But the expression **testing** or "proving," in the opinion of most modern commentators, rather means the "genuineness" (what is left as the real thing after the testing has taken place) instead of the **testing** itself. This is undoubtedly the meaning of this word in 1 Peter 1:7 and could be the meaning here. Moffatt translates: "The sterling temper of your faith produces endurance." But Arndt and Gingrich and the majority of the newer translators (e.g., Phillips, Goodspeed, and NEB) hold to the more traditional rendering. The meaning "genuineness" would give the following sense: "Count it joy when you are tempted, since you may recognize that what is genuine in your faith will produce steadfastness." If our faith is genuine, we can not only stand the trial, but we will be stronger for the experience. On this basis the occasions of trial may be considered a joy. But the other meaning of **testing** or "trial" can also make good sense. The trying of faith produces patience because faith (assuming that it is genuine) can be strengthened by such experiences, and greater loyalty and fidelity to God will be wrought in us. In either case the trial results in **steadfastness** in the true believer.

Steadfastness is better than "patience." The word means "endurance," or "perseverance." Notice Romans 2:7 and 2 Corinthians 6:4. Other scriptures which stress this need of **steadfastness** are Hebrews 10:36; 12:1; Luke 21:19. Many of the Jews considered this quality the queen of the virtues. In view of the long-suffering which the nation had undergone, this is understandable. Persecutions were new to the Gentile Christians, but the Jews were long-suffering. When the Christian's faith is what it ought to be, the difficulties of life

Perfect and Complete — JAMES 1:4

⁴And let steadfastness have its full effect, that you may be perfect and complete, lacking in nothing.

---

only make him both desire and be enabled to continue. A muscle is strengthened and hardened by strenuous labor. The more the runner trains and punishes himself the more likely he is of winning. This is the "knowledge" or "recognition" which James calls for in such trials. It is this which can enable him to treat trials as joys.

[4] Steadfastness is to have its **full effect. Effect** here means "manifestation" or "practical proof" (cf. "work of faith" in 1 Thess. 1:3, i.e., faith manifested in work). Thus James says that this **steadfastness** or patience must be put to actual work; it must be allowed to work in our lives in the midst of trials. Goodspeed translates: "Steadfastness must have full play." Arndt and Gingrich translate: "Let endurance show itself perfectly in practice."

James sees the chance that some may lose heart amid struggles; but these never become **perfect;** that is, they do not attain the end or stature which God intends for them. They fall short or are **lacking. Perfect and complete** does not mean moral perfection or sinlessness. The idea is that patience allows one to fulfill his lot as a Christian, to attain to the station or stature to which God has called him. NEB renders "You will go on to complete a balanced character that will fall short in nothing."

The one who has genuine faith amid persecutions and difficulties finds endurance developed in himself. "We rejoice in our sufferings knowing that suffering produces endurance [**steadfastness**], and endurance produces character, and character produces hope" (Rom. 5:3, 4).

The word **complete** is used of that which has no blemishes and is complete in all parts. It is often used to describe sacrifices which meet all the requirements of the ritual. The noun form is used of the lame man healed by Peter and John (Acts 3:16). Hermas uses it of faith that is intact or blameless (*Mandates* V.ii.3). Here it has the sense of a character that meets all the requirements of maturity.

Lacking in nothing is the equivalent of completeness.

James does not teach moral perfection or sinlessness, but the reaching of the desired goal—full growth or maturity of character. James will say later (3:2), "We all make many mistakes." Sinlessness is not the meaning of "sanctification" in the New Testament, though this is the goal toward which all should aspire. The fulness of God (Eph. 3:19) or the measure of the stature of Christ (Eph. 4:13) must be our aim. The idea of an entire sanctification by the Holy Spirit as a second work of grace is not a biblical idea. The New Testament teaching is that of a progressive perfecting of holiness (2 Cor. 7:1) through daily renewal (2 Cor. 4:16). The rendering of the NEB in Matthew 5:48 ("You must be all goodness, just as your heavenly Father is all good.") is certainly not supported by anything in the context of the passage. Since the context is that of complete love—for both just and unjust, the perfection is that of the perfect love which characterizes the Father. James uses the word **perfect** again (3:2) of the man able to bridle the whole body. Its basic meaning is that of maturity of character. See Colossians 1:28; 4:12; 1 Corinthians 14:20; Hebrews 5:12-14; and Philippians 3:15.

Wisdom in Trials, 1:5-8

Verse 5 begins a subsection in which "wisdom" is stressed. James connects the thought by picking up the word "lacks" in the previous verse, as he had done with steadfastness in verses 3 and 4. There is much discussion as to whether in such passages one is to consider this a new subject or a part of the larger context of the subject "trials." Some contend that James simply strings subjects together like pearls or beads on a string and no connection should be sought. But a deeper study of the whole section seems to indicate that throughout verses 2-18 the general subject is pursued. In verse 12 James returns to the subject of trials (as though summarizing). Hence it is better (and certainly does no violence) to connect wisdom and poverty with trials. The thought is elliptical and is to be understood something as follows: If anyone lacks wisdom to see the value and ability in trials as just explained, he must go to a divine source for such wisdom. He should ask of God.

Wisdom — JAMES 1:5

⁵**If any of you lacks wisdom, let him ask God, who gives to all men generously and without reproaching, and it will be given him.**

[5] What is **wisdom**? It is not mere knowledge. Knowledge comes from experience, particularly through the revelation of God and our study and learning of it. But one may be a "walking Bible" and not be wise. Nor does it mean knowledge gained by direct revelation. This was the mistake made by Joseph Smith, the founder of Mormonism. He read this promise and decided to pray for a revelation, which he claimed he got. Wisdom is the common sense to put into practice the principles and instructions given in the revelation of God's word. The man who believes in God, who fears or reverences him, and who lets his will have its way in his life is wise, but "the fool despises instruction."

The Jews, as many other people of the Near East, had a special interest in wise sayings. Wisdom writing was one genre of their literature. But the Jews grounded their wisdom literature on the revelation of God's word. Notice that in the book of Proverbs, especially in the first chapters, wisdom is personified. She speaks to man to inform him what is good for him. Hort says that the sense of the word is "that endowment of heart and mind which is needed for the right conduct of life." Proverbs, Psalms, Job, and Ecclesiastes, as well as the Jewish apocryphal books of Sirach and the Wisdom of Solomon, are examples of wisdom literature. Job shares with James the thought that wisdom is needed to develop the right attitude toward suffering.

There is a sense in which **wisdom** is the central emphasis of the book of James. Mayor says that James gives it the emphasis which Paul gives to faith, Peter to hope, and John to love. James elaborates on "wisdom from above" in 3:13-18.

James knows that in the midst of trials no matter how well Christians may know God's will they will face circumstances which demand that they be "wise as serpents and harmless as doves." He gives the answer to those who feel the lack of wisdom. In all areas of Christian conduct there is need for wisdom and for remembering its source.

The source of wisdom is God, and the method of obtaining it is prayer. Notice the reflection of Jesus' words in the Sermon on the Mount: "Ask, and it will be given you" (Matt. 7:7). Prayers for wisdom are frequent in Jewish literature: 1 Kings 3:5-15; 4:29-34; Proverbs 2:6; Wisdom 7:7; 9:4.

God gave Solomon wisdom in answer to his prayer. No other will ever attain the stature of wisdom which he had (1 Kings 3:12). God will still give wisdom to all who ask, and in a generous quantity. The word for **generously** is difficult to translate, for it can mean many things. Sometimes it seems to mean "simply" or "singly," that is, without any conditions or strings attached. In *Barnabas* 6:5 "to write simply" means to write plainly. Again, it seems to be equivalent to our word "liberally," since the gift which is willing and unconditional tends also to be liberal. Consider 2 Corinthians 8:2; 9:11; and Romans 12:8. The "sound eye" (Matt. 6:22; Luke 11:34) seems to mean "generous," as opposed to the "unsound" or evil eye which means "stingy": Matthew 20:15; Mark 7:22. So the meaning here seems to be that God is lavish in his gifts, especially in the giving of wisdom. God as Father knows how to do exceedingly abundantly above all that we ask or think. Thus the man who desires, asks for, and seeks wisdom throughout a life of patience and steadfastness may expect to receive it.

It is interesting to note that the description of God as the one **who gives** is so placed in Greek as to be a direct modifier or attribute: "Let him ask of the giving God." It is the very nature of God to give, just as it is for him to love and forgive. We need not worry as to how God will impart that wisdom. If we ask, he will give.

God does not reproach or upbraid the one to whom he has given. Some give so that they may remind the one who has received of their generosity and his debt. Sirach has the following, which may be what James (who certainly must have known the book) is thinking of: "My son, do not mix reproach with your good deeds, nor cause grief by your words when you present a gift. . . . Indeed, does not a word surpass a good gift? . . . and the gift of a grudging man makes the

Ask in Faith — JAMES 1:6

⁶But let him ask in faith, with no doubting, for he who doubts is like a wave of the sea that is driven and tossed by the wind.

---

eyes dim" (Sirach 18:15-18). From the same book we have, "Do not upbraid after making a gift" (41:22). No one likes a gift given so that the giver can parade his liberality.

[6] Jesus said that **faith** is a condition of acceptable prayer (Mark 11:23). To pray **in faith** means to pray in the trust that God will answer the prayer according to his will. We are not only to believe that God exists but also that "he rewards those who seek him" (Heb. 11:6). There have always been materialists who doubt the power of God to answer prayer in a world of science. But law and order answer to the lawgiver. Others doubt the goodness of God or his disposition to bless us. Is it not strange that the Father of our Lord Jesus Christ should be thought of as a harsh God? What is needed is belief and trust in God, not an "understanding" of all God's ways in the universe.

The classical meaning of the verb **doubting** is "to divide, to make a distinction, judge, or dispute," but the meaning "doubt," "be at odds with one's self," appears in the New Testament (Matt. 21:21; Mark 11:23; Rom. 4:20; 14:23; Jude 22; cf. "hesitation" in Acts 10:20). The KJV's "wavering" blends in the context with the figure of the wave of the sea. This **doubting** shows that the praying person has not committed himself fully to trust in God. The same word is used by James in 2:4 and in 4:3f. In the latter passage it is indecision between friendship with God and the world.

The doubting petitioner is changing and uncertain **like a wave of the sea.** The word for **wave** means the "billows, the rough water, the breakers" upon the shore. The word is used elsewhere in the New Testament only in Luke 8:24, of the waves of the storm on the Sea of Galilee. When the surf is wind-driven and tossed, it is then really raging. The whole picture is one of indecision, of uncertainty. Perhaps the thought is that the one praying is lifted high like the crest of the wave by hope one minute and then lowered by doubt and despair of receiving the next (cf. Eph. 4:13, 14).

JAMES 1:7, 8 — *Double-minded*

7,8 For that person must not suppose that a double-minded man, unstable in all his ways, will receive anything from the Lord.

[7, 8] Except one pray in faith, that one need not even think to receive. **That person** is the doubter, and there is something of contempt in the expression, as though a doubting, halting man of prayer is a contradiction. The verb **suppose** is used in the Septuagint (Gen. 37:7) of what Joseph supposed in his dream.

A double-minded man is not found in biblical texts outside of James' use here and in 4:8. But in later ecclesiastical Greek it is a frequent word occurring in the adjective form, as a verb meaning "to hesitate," or "be double-minded," and in the noun form meaning "indecision, doubt, or hesitancy." In *1 Clement* 11:2 we have: "For the doubters and the uncertain about the power of God are for judgment." The *Didache* mentions the sin of double-mindedness as a part of the way of death. As already noted, James uses this word again in 4:8 of the man who would serve God and the world at the same time. Both uses portray men who act as if they had two minds and thought with both at the same time (cf. Sirach 2:12, "Woe . . . to the sinner who walks along two ways").

The doubter is **unstable** or restless. In 3:8 James uses the same word of the tongue; it is a "restless" evil, that is, a continual, neverceasing evil. Here the idea is unsettled, fickle, and, hence, unreliable. Such a man cannot be trusted.

In all his ways means in his paths. The word in the plural often means conduct as a whole (cf. Acts 14:16 and Rom. 3:16). The usage is a frequent Old Testament one: Proverbs 3:1 and 6; Psalm 10:5; Jeremiah 16:17. In 1:11 the word is different and means "undertakings, pursuits, or schemes." Goodspeed renders it "uncertain about everything he does." The NEB reads: "Can never keep a steady course."

The Lord here is probably the Father, inasmuch as the prayer for wisdom is to be directed to him. But the same expression in 5:14 probably refers to Jesus. One who prays in doubt may receive God's blessings in natural ways, but his prayers are not answered.

Riches   JAMES 1:9, 10

⁹Let the lowly brother boast in his exaltation, ¹⁰and the rich in his humiliation, because like the flower of the grass he will pass away.

The Trials of Poverty and Riches, 1:9-11

James progresses to a new phase of the subject. The verb "boast" is set forward emphatically in the sentence, probably because of its similarity to the word "joy" in verse 2. It expresses a Christian's continued confidence in any circumstance in which he finds himself. Also it is a contrast to the doubting, hesitant man of the previous section. The general idea of the section is that of Proverbs 22:2: "The rich and the poor meet together; the Lord is the maker of them all." The poor is not to be depressed by the trial of poverty, nor the rich proud of his wealth. Life is uncertain. The gospel teaches each person to make adjustment to a new and common station in Christ, and each in turn can find something to boast of in what Christianity has done for him.

[9, 10] There has been much discussion as to whether both of those addressed in the section are to be thought of as Christians. James uses the term **brother** in the first case but not in the second. Some take the position that the teachings of the gospel assume that no rich man can be a Christian. But this position is certainly false. Many of Jesus' friends and early disciples were well-to-do: Joseph of Arimathea, Barnabas, Nicodemus, Mary (sister of Lazarus), and the women of Galilee. James would hardly have written in the supposition that no rich were potential Christians. In 2:6 he does speak of the rich as a class in a derogatory manner, but this is to be explained on the grounds that this was the general rule, to which the devoted and humble Christian among the rich is the exception.

In his teaching on the uncertainty of riches James is reflecting the teaching of Jesus: Matthew 6:19-34; 19:16-30; Luke 12:15-21; 16:9-31; Mark 10:24; and compare 1 Corinthians 7:29-31; 1 Timothy 6:17.

The gulf between the rich and poor in New Testament times was great—greater perhaps than in our modern times. There was no large middle class with its abundance due to industrial jobs. The poor were despised and often oppressed (James 5:1ff.). There was in the possession of riches a constant source of pride. The desire for money under such circumstances would be keen (1 Tim. 6:9).

As in Luke 1:52, the word **lowly** here means "poor" in terms of wealth. In other passages, such as 4:6, the word is a character trait; so also in Romans 12:16. The rich man is set over against the word in the next verse, showing that material poverty is the meaning here.

James' statements in this section are capable of being interpreted in several ways, as a check of several commentaries or even of translations will reveal. The descriptive phrases following the word **boast** are nouns standing in prepositional phrases: **in his exaltation** and **in his humiliation.** In each case some would read into these a temporal relation and translate "when he is raised" (Moffatt) and "when he is brought low." Taken in this way, the admonition is that the Christian is to do his duty in whatever circumstances the changing fortunes of life may thrust upon him. If the poor should become rich, he is to accept the fact without exulting or taking pride in it; if the rich man, on the other hand, should lose his money and become poor, let him boast or glory in his poor estate, since riches are notoriously fleeting.

Another possibility is that the phrases are to be taken as irony: the rich man who now boasts in his wealth is to boast (if he can when it happens) in the poverty which is coming upon him. This would be as if James says, "Your wealth is soon to be taken away; then we'll see if you can boast."

It is better, however, to take the words as they stand to mean that in whichever of the two states one finds himself, there is something of which he may *at that time* boast: if poor—in the wealth of his station in Christ; if rich—in the position of humility which he is to assume in the church in spite of his riches. Phillips puts it: "The brother who is poor may be glad because God has called him to the true riches. The rich may be glad because God has shown him his spiritual poverty."

Boast

The word **boast** in the sense of glory or take pride in (in a good sense) is common in the New Testament, and Paul is especially fond of it. A check of the concordance reveals that Paul uses it of glorying in God or Christ (Rom. 5:11; 15:17; 1 Cor. 1:31; Phil. 3:3), in the cross (Gal. 6:14), in the hope of salvation (Rom. 5:2), in those he had converted (2 Thess. 1:4, etc.), in affliction (Rom. 5:3), and in infirmities (2 Cor. 12:9). Paul feels foolish for glorying in his accomplishments in answer to his critics (2 Cor. 11:16ff.). Boasting in the law (Rom. 2:17), in self-righteousness (Rom. 3:27), in the mistake of a fellow Christian (1 Cor. 5:6), or in racial advantages (Gal. 6:13) is condemned. James uses the term in 4:16 in a bad sense. Here the poor may **boast** in his attainment in Christ. He need not be ashamed of his poverty; he has something which balances it.

The word **exaltation** can mean "pride," and, in a concrete usage in the plural, "the heavens." But here it means "high position" or "rank" (cf. Luke 1:52 and Job 5:11). The verb is used in the frequently quoted paradox: "The one who humbles himself shall be exalted" (Luke 14:11; 18:14). The Christian's spiritual condition is one of richness, of **exaltation** in Christ. He is priest and king (Rev. 1:6; 5:10; 1 Peter 2:9). He is to participate with Christ in judgment (1 Cor. 6:3). His spiritual blessings constitute promises "precious and very great" (2 Peter 1:4). Christ became poor that we might be made rich (2 Cor. 8:9). Compare Hebrews 11:26; Philippians 4:19; Ephesians 3:8. Though the world may scorn the Christian, he is heir of all God's honor, glory, and wealth. In all this he may take pride.

James says that **the rich** should boast in his humble station as a Christian. The world looks on a Christian as a nobody. The rich man's fellows would probably belittle his faith. He himself has voluntarily taken on the attitude of a servant (James 4:10). He may accept the fact that his wealth counts for nothing and challenge even the poor to be more humble than he. Jesus taught: "Let the leader become as one who serves" (Luke 22:26). Compare the attitude of Paul in Philippians 3:5-8. If the rich should lose his wealth, he may take it joyfully (Heb. 10:34), but this is not James' point here.

JAMES 1:10, 11 — Pass Away

11For the sun rises with its scorching heat and withers the grass; its flower falls, and its beauty perishes. So will the rich man fade away in the midst of his pursuits.

Like the flower of the grass the rich man is soon to **pass away**. He is here today but gone tomorrow. In James 4:14 to the rich merchant who is presumptuous in planning his future he says, "You are a mist that appears for a little time and then vanishes." It is not the wealth itself that James sees as fleeting (though it is certainly that) but the life of the rich. Palestine has two rainy seasons. After the spring rains, the grass grows profusely; but after they cease the flower soon disappears (cf. Matt. 13:6). The expression **pass away** for death and disappearance is not uncommon (cf. Matt. 24:34, "This generation will not pass away"). For the figure compare "My heart is smitten like grass and withered" (Ps. 102:4) and also Isaiah 40:6 (of fleeting human life), which is quoted in full in 1 Peter 1:24 (cf. also Ps. 37:2; Job 14:2).

Life is as fleeting for the poor man as for the rich, but James' warning here is directed toward the rich, because the tendency to trust in the uncertainty of riches may make him more likely to forget the fact. If only one's wealth recommends him, then when it is gone he has nothing to boast of. Thus James is saying that the rich should glory in his self-abasement, in that which some would consider as worthless, but which is for him the earnest of his eternal inheritance. Quickly he will pass from this life, leaving behind his earthly wealth (1 Tim. 6:7) in which most rich people glory. Hence he should boast in the things that are more abiding.

[11] The verbs here represent what customarily or repeatedly happens. The hot **sun** beams down on the **grass** after the rains cease. The **grass** does not last long in the summer. The word **grass** is usually used of green grass of the meadow (Matt. 14:19). But here it must include also flowering plants as growing together. The verb **falls** refers to the falling of the petals of flowers. Even Jesus remarked about the **beauty** of the flowers (Matt. 6:28, 29) as well as of the fact that the flower is "alive today and tomorrow is thrown into the oven."

Fade Away JAMES 1:11, 12

¹²**Blessed is the man who endures trial, for when he has stood the test he will receive the crown of life which God has promised to those who love him.**

Riches may be lost as suddenly as the **flower falls.** But whether wealth is lost or not, the individual is mortal and will not remain. Man must put his confidence in something more permanent than riches. The verb **fade away** is used of the withering of flowers (Job 15:30), of the fading of beauty, and elsewhere of the untimely death of a loved one. The word in a negative form ("unfading") furnished the name of an evergreen plant used by Peter (1 Peter 5:4) to typify the crown of life. Either in his **pursuits** of business (trade journeys, 4:13) or (more likely) in his busy **pursuits** and customs of life, he is suddenly gone.

James' point in this discussion is that, though wealth is to be thought of from a worldly viewpoint as a trial, the Christian may view it otherwise. The poor is thus not to bemoan his fate or the rich take pride in his wealth. It is quite possible that the subject of partiality toward the rich at the expense of the poor in 2:1ff. may be connected with this passage. The thoughts certainly are parallel. If Christians are judging their poor brethren as described, they are certainly not considering the "exaltation" or "high estate" of the poor brother in Christ.

This verse seems to complete the thought begun in verse 2 of finding joy in the midst of trials. It also forms the transition to the next section. James has asserted that trials are a joy in that they are intended to work in us the spirit of patient endurance. Now James further promises that they become a beatitude because the one enduring them will, when he is approved, be awarded a crown.

Patient Endurance in Trials Rewarded, 1:12

[12] The word **blessed** could be translated "happy," or "fortunate." In a religious setting it probably suggests something of the life or condition apart from the world's ills, for it denoted to the Greeks the kind of life the immortal gods lived. (Compare 1 Tim. 1:11; 6:15—the only instances in the New Testament where it refers to God.)

JAMES 1:12 *Endurance*

The same Greek words for **Blessed is the man who endures** occur in the Septuagint of Daniel 12:12, which James may have remembered. The endurance is in bearing or suffering temptation and remaining faithful. This does not necessarily mean that one must always overcome in a trial or that one can never err in a trial. But since errors must be corrected and repented of, some who backslide never recover. One must never be overcome and give up. "By your endurance you will gain your lives" (Luke 21:19). The reason for the blessedness is stated in the closing part of this verse—the reward of the crown. This result is restated in James 5:11 in different terms.

The Greek word rendered **stood the test** means that something has been tried and proved genuine; hence, as in Romans 16:10 ("Greet Apelles who is approved in Christ"), it means "the tried and true Christian." Compare also 1 Corinthians 11:19; 2 Corinthians 10:18; 13:7; 2 Timothy 2:15. When the Christian endures the trials which come his way—neither growing weary and quitting nor being fatally captured by Satan through his wiles, thus being perfected and strengthened by successive triumphs—he will receive the reward. God is not unwilling that we should be tested in this way. The Spirit was the agent of Jesus' being driven out into the wilderness to be tempted by the devil (Mark 1:12). This knowledge of the use of trials leads the Christian to joy in meeting them.

The Greek word for **crown** is the source of our name "Stephen." The crown was usually made of leaves. Jesus' was of thorns (Matt. 27:29). The wreath was worn by the victor at athletic contests (1 Cor. 9:25), at festivals (Isa. 28:1f.), and also at times by kings and dignitaries as a sign of rank (so Christ in Rev. 14:14). But the usual headdress of an Eastern ruler was a purple band trimmed with white on a tiara, the diadem. The term **crown** is often used figuratively of a virtue or reward: "fair garland for your head" (Prov. 1:9) or "beautiful crown" (Prov. 4:9). So here **crown of life** means the crown which consists of life (Matt. 7:14), that is, immortality. The **crown of life** in this verse is not to be confused with the new life in Christ which is described as the

Temptation JAMES 1:12, 13

¹³Let no one say when he is tempted, "I am tempted by God"; for God cannot be tempted with evil and he himself tempts no one;

---

promise of the Christian in this world (Rom. 6:4; cf. 2 Tim. 1:1; 2 Cor. 5:17; Gal. 6:15; Eph. 4:23f.; John 10:10).

Promises of blessings on those who love God are frequent in both the Old Testament and the New: Exodus 20:6; Psalm 5:11; 1 Corinthians 2:9 (here Paul has quoted the Septuagint, Isa. 64:4, though the Greek translation differs somewhat from Paul); 1 Corinthians 8:3. Jesus had taught that keeping his word was evidence of love for him (John 14:23; 15:10). **Love** is conceived as the motivating power which makes endurance possible.

Temptations Not from God, 1:13-16

What James has said about trials might be used by some to blame God for the temptations which are the occasions for their sins. In Greek the same word is rendered "trial" and "temptation." Only the context will indicate which of the meanings is present. In these verses James is guarding against a misapplication of his teaching in the section on trials. God does not tempt people to do wrong.

[13] The term "trial" in verse 2 and "temptation" are from an action noun formation in Greek, while the word in this verse is a verb from the same root. It is much discussed as to whether the sense of the words is the same or not. The consensus of commentators seems to be that James' habit of taking up the words used previously as the leading idea of the new section shows that James has reference to a common conception, though with a double sense. The noun has reference to the objective trial, the verb to the subjective temptation. Here, then, James is dealing with the inner yielding of the man to inducement to sin which may accompany the outward trial designed by God for man's good. Man is not to think that because God permits him to be tested he is therefore to blame if he yields to an urge to sin which Satan may present on the occasion. Several commentators cite a parallel in Sirach 15:11ff., "Do not say, 'Because of the Lord I

JAMES 1:13, 14 — *God and Temptation*

¹⁴but each person is tempted when he is lured and enticed by his own desire.

left the right way'; for he will not do what he hates. Do not say 'It was he who led me astray'; for he has no need of a sinful man. The Lord hates all abominations, and they are not loved by those who fear him." **When he is tempted** is a participle in Greek, "while being tempted." In the course of temptation one should not excuse himself into yielding by thinking that he can blame another.

Some Jews blamed God for sin. They observed an evil tendency in man, which they called *yetzer hara*. There was an argument over the origin of this tendency. Some argued that Satan put the tendency in man; others said man alone was responsible. But it was boldly reasoned by some that God created all things and so he must have created the evil in man. If true, this would make God responsible for man's sin.

Cannot be tempted is not found elsewhere in either the Septuagint or the New Testament. This passage confirms the conclusion that "temptation" here means seduction to do evil. The truth expressed is that God's nature is such that he is not susceptible to evil or sin. Bible writers affirm the absolute holiness of God. He is love (thus above hate in its moral sense); he cannot lie (Titus 1:2); he is a God of holiness (1 Peter 1:15).

The argument is that, since God is completely free from the power of temptation, it is also beyond his nature to tempt others. That would in itself be an evil. The **himself** may emphasize that God is not personally responsible for enticement to sin. There is a sense in which one might say that God is indirectly responsible for such, since he may ordain an incident of testing which the devil may use to seduce one to sin. But even here God is not responsible for sin. He works in such instances to counteract the work of the enemy. Paul tells us, "He will not let you be tempted beyond your strength, but with the temptation will also provide the way of escape, that you may be able to endure it" (1 Cor. 10:13).

[14] The possibility of temptation and sin is universal. The Bible knows nothing of the idea of entire sanctification

Lured by Desire

wherein one rises above the possibility of sin by the eradication of evil tendency in himself. "If we say that we have no sin, we deceive ourselves, and the truth is not in us" (1 John 1:8). Even the Son of God was tempted in every respect as we are (Heb. 4:15). Paul said that he had to pommel his body and subdue it (1 Cor. 9:27).

The verb **lured** means to be "dragged or taken in tow by." This is a strong word to express the intensity of the lusts or passions in us. Compare Paul's equally strong language in Romans 7:5, 18-24. The law of sin in our members leads us to do evil while our minds will to do what is good. The situation led Paul to describe himself as a "wretched man." The same lusts are described by James later (4:1) as at war in our members. James emphasizes that it is by our own desires (cf. 2 Tim. 4:3; 2 Peter 3:3; Jude 18f.), rather than by God, that we are tempted. The origin of temptation is within. Satan is bound as far as we are concerned (Matt. 12:29; Heb. 2:14) and has no power over us that we do not give him (1 Cor. 10:13). His enticements would have no power unless something within us were appealed to by his temptation. There would be no temptation to gluttony or fornication if there were no appetites for food or sex. Certain desires are stronger in some than in others. One may be strongly influenced by strong drink; for another, drink may have no enticement. Satan searches out the weak spot in our members.

The term **desire** is a neutral term in its predominant use in secular authors. In the Bible it may have a good sense, as in Proverbs 10:24 ("The desire of the righteous"); Philippians 1:23; and 1 Thessalonians 2:17. In a bad sense (as here) it means a desire to do what is forbidden, especially in respect to the lower desire of the flesh. For this use, especially of illicit sexual desire, see Romans 7:7f.; Colossians 3:5; 1 Thessalonians 4:5; Galatians 5:24; 1 Peter 4:3; 1 Timothy 6:9; 2 Timothy 2:22; 4:3; 2 Peter 2:10; Ephesians 4:22. Every honest man's conscience bears witness to his responsibility for sin. Like David he must confess, "I know my transgressions, and my sin is ever before me" (Ps. 51:3). Thousands rise above their circumstances. Man falls, not because of circumstances, but because of yielding to what is within. It is

JAMES 1:15 — *Birth of Sin*

¹⁵Then desire when it has conceived gives birth to sin; and sin when it is full-grown brings forth death.

---

also interesting to note that lusts or desires are personified in the passage.

The verb **enticed** originally was used of the devices of the hunter. But it came to be associated with the wiles of the evil woman. Second Peter 2:14, 18 warns of false teachers who "entice unsteady souls" and even pictures how it is done.

[15] Desire is personified as an enticing woman. **Sin** is the child of the surrender of the will to the allurements of desire. It may be argued, as some have done, that Satan is really the father of sin. But James is using allegory, and in the allegory he takes the figure only back as far as the desire of the one seduced. For the word **conceived** James uses the regular Greek word for a woman's conception in childbirth (cf. Gen. 4:1; 30:17; Luke 1:24, where the Septuagint and Luke use the same word). The Septuagint in Psalm 7:14 has a similar use of the metaphor: "He hath travailed with unrighteousness, he has conceived affliction and brought forth iniquity." For the taking of the thought further back to Satan, compare the Jewish treatise the *Testaments of the Twelve Patriarchs* (*Benjamin* 7:2), "The mind conceives through Beliar (Satan)." Justin Martyr says in the *Dialogue with Trypho,* "Eve when a virgin conceived the disobedient word from the serpent and bore death" (ch. 100).

Gives birth is one of the ordinary words in Greek for the birth of young (Matt. 1:21, of Jesus' birth). The figure of birth is continued in the word **full-grown.** In this context the sense of the word is that of full age or maturity. Sin does not result in death immediately, nor does it necessarily do so. Repentance and confession (1 John 1:7-9; Acts 8:22) may avoid the result of sin. But if sin is allowed to grow unchecked and to become perfected in our lives without repentance, it will produce ruin.

Brings forth is used in the New Testament only here and in verse 18 of this same chapter. The figure is not completely carried through. There is no mention of the conception of sin before bearing death. But the child sin, when grown, has the

Death JAMES 1:15-17

¹⁶**Do not be deceived, my beloved brethren. ¹⁷Every good endowment and every perfect gift is from above, coming down from the Father of lights with whom there is no variation or shadow due to change.**ᵃ

ᵃOther ancient authorities read *variation due to a shadow of turning*

---

power to produce death, as lust has to bring sin into a life. The fact emphasized is a common one in Scripture: "The wages of sin is death" (Rom. 6:23; 8:6). Matthew 7:13, 14 mentions the fatal consequences of following the wrong way.

Death does not mean merely physical death, since all will die that death (though sin does at times result in physical death). Nor does James mean merely that men become "dead to what is good" ("dead through trespasses and sins," Eph. 2:1ff.). The death meant is eternal death, the second death (cf. Heb. 6:6 and 1 John 5:16). The Bible does teach that a child of God can so sin as to be finally lost. The climax of James' reasoning is thus reached in showing that the final result of temptation is death. But God is the giver of life and could not be charged with being guilty of the death of those to whom he wills only what is good.

[16] Do not be deceived about the source of temptation. The verse is to be connected in this way with the preceding thought. Good gifts (as James will go on to say), not evil ones, come from God. Let no one therefore deceive you into yielding to the impulses to sin by laying the blame on God. **Brethren,** as so often, softens the zeal of James' language. Such warnings against our being deceived are numerous: Luke 21:8; 1 Corinthians 6:9; 15:33; Galatians 6:7.

This verse is intended to be connected with the subject discussed in verses 13 to 15. Though some would charge that God is the source of allurements to do evil, these are wrong. Anyone accepting this conclusion is allowing himself to be deceived. God's gifts fall only in the class of good things.

The True Nature of God's Giving, 1:17, 18

[17] James uses two different words for **gift.** In form the first (**endowment**) means the "act of giving" itself (as in Phil. 4:15, where it is contrasted with the act of "receiving"), and the second means the result of the giving, "the gift" itself (Rom. 5:16). The adjective **good** probably here means "useful," or "beneficial," as in Ephesians 4:29; while **perfect** means "what has attained its purpose or end," hence "complete" or without defect. Thus James emphasizes that "every useful act of giving" and all complete or perfect benefits are from God.

When James emphasizes that "every" good and perfect gift is from God, the context demands that James means that God is the ultimate giver of such gifts and that he gives only such things as may be so described. This could mean that some things might seem to be bad (in the limitation of human wisdom) and still come from God. But it denies that what is positively evil (like inducement to sin) can be attributed to him. We are taught that God's philanthropy is responsible for all we have (Acts 17:28, 29).

From above refers to heaven, the dwelling place of God (Acts 14:17; John 19:11; 3:31). God is creator of heaven and earth and as such is the father of all heavenly bodies—the sun, moon, and stars. But there is a double meaning to the words. These **lights** symbolize spiritual light, as in John 1:4, 5; 8:12ff.; 9:5. God is the originator of all light, both physical and spiritual. Notice that in the next verse the blessing that is spelled out as the specific illustration of God's grace to us is the privilege of becoming his children. The following passages refer to God as creator of the **lights:** Genesis 1:14; Jeremiah 4:23; 31:35; Psalm 136:7, besides Jewish sources.

The noun **variation** is a rare word for astronomical changing. The reference is probably to the rising and setting of the sun (as we think of it), or to the waning and waxing of the moon, and also possibly to the instability of the lesser lights. God is the father of such lights, but in his giving of good things he is not constantly changing. His gifts are always good, perfect, and abundant. They are not withheld even because of our lack of constancy. In giving wisdom (1:5ff.) and in his giving spiritual illumination, as well as physical blessings, he is a consistent giver. The next verse will bring out the point further.

Unvarying Goodness JAMES 1:17, 18

¹⁸Of his own will he brought us forth by the word of truth that we should be a kind of first fruits of his creatures.

The text as adopted by most modern editors is literally "There is no variation or a shadow of turning." There are several other readings in the different manuscripts. The difference is mainly between **variation** or "turning **shadow**" (two things, as in the text) and "variation which consists of turning shadow" (one thing, as in the note). The textual differences undoubtedly exist because the scribes have tried to clear up what seemed to them a puzzling expression. Whichever reading is adopted, James' point is that God created the lights, but they are changing and varying. But God himself, the father of the lights, is not like the lights he created. Light from him is constant and steady. God so consistently gives good things that he could not be the author of evil temptations.

[18] James concludes the thought begun in verse 12: Our participation in the new birth, the privilege of being children of God, is an example of God's gracious gifts in contrast to the thought that he is the source of temptation to sin and death.

Of his own will emphasizes the thought that our salvation is the result of the deliberate choice and purpose of God, that is, that it is a gracious gift from him. Our salvation grew out of his desire, good pleasure, and counsel alone. It was his will, free from any outside necessity or cause. This is in harmony with the general teaching of the Bible that salvation is a free gift—a matter of unmerited favor, springing from the fountain of God's love.

As sin begat death (vs. 15), so God our Father **brought us forth** as his children. The **us** refers, not to men in general, but to Christians. Christians are born of the will of God (John 1:13). Many New Testament passages speak of the rebirth of souls dead in trespasses and sins through the gospel: 1 Peter 1:3, 23; 1 John 2:29; 3:19; 4:7f.; 5:1; 1 Corinthians 4:15; John 3:5. The use of the aorist tense (of point action in past time) seems to refer to a definite act in our lives—our conversion, culminating in our baptism into the new life (Rom. 6:4; John

3:5). The efforts of some commentators to make the words refer to creation (Gen. 1:26) are hardly successful. The **word of truth** as the instrument of God's "bringing us forth" is not the statement "Let us make man," but the gospel of Jesus Christ. Compare the continued use of this **word of truth** which we are to receive with meekness (vss. 19ff.). The use of the term **first fruits** of us as Christians (man was not the first fruits of the world's creation) and the clear implication of the following verses that James is speaking of the "salvation of our souls through the word" (vs. 21) make it plain that the birth is the new birth.

The **word** or message conveys the **truth** of God (compare other passages where the possessive genitive sustains a similar relation to the noun: Col. 1:5, "The word of truth of the Gospel"; Acts 13:26, "The word of this salvation"; and 2 Tim. 2:15, "rightly handling the word of truth"). As in these passages, the **word of truth** here is the gospel as God's revelation or proclamation by which the world is regenerated through Christ. With this, consider 1 Peter 1:23 and 1 Corinthians 4:15. No explanation of the new birth is scripturally sound that makes it independent of the preached word and obedience to the ordinances of that word (Matt. 28:19, 20; Acts 2:38; 22:16; 1 Peter 3:21; Mark 16:16). The idea of a direct operation of the Spirit, acting in some mysterious way apart from the **word of truth,** is not a Bible idea. A confidence that one is "saved" gained from some subjective feeling apart from obedience to God's word is not the assurance that the New Testament gives of pardon (1 John 2:3).

A kind of means "not a literal first fruits" in the Old Testament sense, but **first fruits** in another, or spiritual, sense. The first fruit was the first portion of produce (animal or plant) which belonged to God and was offered to him before the rest could be put to ordinary use. It was to be of the choicest part of the harvest and thus a pledge of further harvest. The law governing it is found in Deuteronomy 18:4; Numbers 18:12; Exodus 13:11-16 (of the firstborn). Israel was so called (Jer. 2:3). The Jewish writer Philo called Israel the first fruit of the whole human race. The idea is that, since Christians, consisting of a portion of the human race, have

First Fruits JAMES 1:18, 19

¹⁹Know this, my beloved brethren. Let every man be quick to hear, slow to speak, slow to anger,

---

been gathered, there is a prediction of the ingathering not only of a larger portion of the Israelites, but of the world's nations into the church (Acts 15:16ff.). There is almost certainly the pledge of holiness also involved. This lies in the idea of not only the first part but the choicest and best part being offered. For other uses in the New Testament compare the following: 1 Corinthians 15:20, 23; Romans 16:5; 1 Corinthians 16:15; in some texts of 2 Thessalonians 2:13; Romans 8:23; and Revelation 14:4 (where, as in our passage in James, the idea is more quality than time). For this idea compare the scholiast on Euripides, *Orestes* 96, "the first fruit means not only the first in rank, but also the first in honor (or preciousness)." The word "firstborn" is a related idea, and for this, see Hebrews 12:23, where Christians are so called. Though **creatures** may involve all creatures including animals (1 Tim. 4:4), it is often limited to mankind (as in Col. 1:23). So the word seems to mean "human beings" here. James sees Christians as the first fruits of the larger number of men.

ATTITUDE TOWARD THE WORD WHICH BEGETS, 1:19-27

This section of James 1 connects with the previous section by the occurrence of the "word of truth." That "word" has been described as the means of God's bringing us forth to be his children. If the word can do so much, then it ought to be accorded the proper attention and response. It must be received with meekness; it must be acted on, being put into active use in a life of benevolence, morality, and self-control. Christians must continue to let God's word be at work in their lives (1 Thess. 2:13).

Meekness in Hearing the Word, 1:19-21

[19] We ought (in view of the word's power) to **be quick to hear**—to be eager and anxious to hear the message of God. Many will listen to the word to be baptized, but not to the

[20] for the anger of man does not work the righteousness of God.

teaching about self-control, good deeds, worshiping God, or other such parts of the doctrine of Christ. Having tasted the "good word of God," Christians ought to be even more eager for it to work in their lives. On the other hand, they should be **slow to speak.** The idea is "slow to speak back at, or show displeasure at the teachings of the word." At Antioch the Jews became jealous and contradicted the word spoken by Paul (Acts 13:45). Some disciples became angry with Paul and became his enemy because he told them the truth about the teaching of Christ (Gal. 4:16). **Slow to anger** means "slow to get angry at the teaching of the word and slow to harbor anger against God." A king in the Bible became so angered at the reading of God's will to him that he cut the page out of the scriptures that the scribe was reading and burned it (Jer. 36).

[20] Man in **anger** cannot please God; in such a state he cannot do works which are acceptable to God. Only those who are humble in spirit can enter his kingdom. Those who would become enraged at the leadings of the Spirit of God in the word as to the kind of lives they should live and the kind of service they should render cannot hope to please him.

One angry at God could or would hardly do or practice the things that God desired him to do. The antithesis of working **righteousness** is doing sin (2:9, where the same verb is used—"commit sin"). **Righteousness** here is not used in the special Pauline sense (Rom. 1:17, 21) of the imputing to us by virtue of the blood of Christ a righteousness which we have not actually attained. Rather the sense here, which is also quite common in Paul (2 Cor. 6:14; 1 Tim. 6:11; 2 Tim. 2:22; Rom. 14:17; Eph. 5:9), as well as elsewhere (Matt. 6:1; 2 Peter 2:21; 1 John 2:29), is that of human works as good deeds which are approved by God, thus "doing right in the sight of God." The word (apart from the special Pauline sense mentioned above) almost always in the New Testament means man's conduct before God, action approved by him. It thus comes to mean virtually uprightness in living. This word always has this sense in Matthew. Thus Jesus is baptized "to fulfil all

Put Away Wickedness JAMES 1:20, 21

²¹Therefore put away all filthiness and rank growth of wickedness and receive with meekness the implanted word, which is able to save your souls.

---

righteousness" (Matt. 3:15), which must mean something like to do all his duty toward God. It is remarkable that James puts it that such deeds cannot be done by human anger. James puts the working of them under the divine and not the human side. Thus we have here a sort of mediating position between Paul's usage and the earlier customary usage.

James implies in the following verse that the primary reason for men's wrath (even that of some Christians) against the teaching of the word is the existence of sins in their lives which they do not wish to correct. The sins are of such nature as those now listed. James throughout the epistle mentions sins of various kinds of which his readers are guilty.

[21] The verb **put away** is the ordinary word for taking off clothes (Acts 7:58). But it is often used (as here) in a figurative sense; for example, Romans 13:12; Colossians 3:8; 1 Peter 2:1.

The term **filthiness** in an ethical sense means "moral uncleanness," "vulgarity," and, in some writers, "avarice or greediness." The more general sense is probably correct here complementing **wickedness.** The force of **all** in such cases is "each instance of" or "every trace of," or perhaps "every kind of." In intent, at least, complete resignation to the will of God is essential. That will dictates a purpose to erase sin from our lives rapidly and in every way possible with God's help. We must not make provision to fulfil the lust of the flesh (Rom. 13:14). Our sins should be those of honest mistake and weakness of the flesh. Sincere repentance envisions nothing else in our lives but to put away all evil. In this way we will perfect sanctification (2 Cor. 7:1). Without this we shall not see God (Heb. 12:14). The word for **rank growth** means "surplus." It implies that such evil is not a normal part of character, but an excess.

The verb **receive** means "to accept" or even "to approve of" (see 1 Cor. 2:14; 2 Cor. 8:17; 2 Thess. 2:10). For the idea of receiving teaching, see Luke 8:13; Acts 8:14; 11:1; 17:11;

1 Thessalonians 1:6; 2:13. Many people are not teachable. The kind of preaching many want to hear is that which confirms their already fixed ideas. Some even resent new insights to old truths. Notice James' implication that even some teachers have too implacable ideas or notions (James 3:17).

Meekness is seen in the Old Testament as the hallmark of the future reign of the Messiah: Psalms 25:9; 34:2; 37:11; 76:9; 147:6; 149:4. The word as an ethical term is concerned with anger; it means "absence from resentment," "resignation in suffering." Here it is opposite to "wrath" and means receiving the word in a yielding and receptive attitude. The word is a key New Testament word. Jesus applied it to himself (Matt. 11:29; see also Matt. 5:4; Col. 3:12; Eph. 4:2; 2 Cor. 10:1; Gal. 5:23; 2 Thess. 3:5).

The **implanted word** has received various translations: Moffatt, "the word which roots itself inwardly"; Goodspeed, "the word planted in your heart"; NEB and Phillips, "the message God has sown in your heart." The word can mean something which is inborn or native to one or something which by absorption becomes deeply rooted and planted in one's being. The word seems to be used here by anticipation: it must be actually received before it can become implanted. Thus the language means "Receive with meekness the word, which, when implanted, can save your soul." There does not seem to be any teaching from the Bible that the word of God is inborn or innate in us, unless one thinks that there are some marks of divine truth in the human conscience and that this might be thought of. The idea of the truth becoming infused and engrafted in our hearts and minds seems to be the correct idea. The word may also be taken as being descriptive or qualitative, meaning the word "whose essence or tendency is to root itself in our hearts" (cf. Matt. 13:21).

God's word is powerful to **save** all, saint and sinner (cf. Rom. 1:16; John 5:24; Luke 1:37; 2 Tim. 2:9). Since these words are addressed to those already born again as God's children, the salvation referred to must be to the future, the culmination of that deliverance already achieved in Christ (2 Thess. 5:23; 2 Peter 1:5). Some would call the use of **souls** here a Hebraism, standing for the whole person, as if he were

Doers of the Word JAMES 1:21, 22

²²But be doers of the word, and not hearers only, deceiving yourselves.

---

saying "is able to save you" (cf. Matt. 11:29; 26:28; 3 John 2; Rev. 18:14). It is possible, however, that James is using the word in a more theological sense of the soul as the seat and center of life which transcends earthly existence (cf. Matt. 10:18; 16:26).

Being Doers of the Word as Well as Hearers, 1:22-25

As James has insisted that we must continue to be good hearers if the word is to save us, so now he also insists that we must be obedient to that word. The word must work effectively in us.

[22] Doers is a characteristic word in James (cf. 1:22, 23, 25; 4:11). In 4:11 it means one who "keeps" or "observes" the law as opposed to one who "judges" the law. Elsewhere in the New Testament the word for "doer" occurs in the classical sense of a "poet" (Acts 17:28). In Romans 2:13 (as here) it is opposed to "mere hearers." James does not mean that his readers are non-Christians who have heretofore been content merely to hear the gospel. Rather he is writing to Christians and stressing their conduct and practice. Some of them are content merely to have become Christians and have not gone on to perfection. The verb which usually means "become" may have the meaning in the present imperative of "go on being or becoming" or "show yourself more and more" (for example, Matt. 10:16; 24:44; 1 Cor. 14:20; 15:28; Eph. 5:1).

The admonition is followed up by James with illustration and explicit examples of what he means. See the references to self-control, good works, and morality at the end of the chapter. Jesus also abhorred the hypocrisy of those who "preach, but do not practice" (Matt. 23:3; cf. 7:21, 24-27; Luke 8:21; John 8:31; 13:17).

In **hearers only** James is not thinking of the reading of the law of Moses in the synagogues, though the complaint was registered that many did only hear the law. He is thinking of Christians who fall short in ways to be mentioned in the book. He thinks of those who hear, read, or study "the perfect

JAMES 1:23, 24 — *Mirror*

²³For if any one is a hearer of the word and not a doer, he is like a man who observes his natural face in a mirror; ²⁴for he observes himself and goes away and at once forgets what he was like.

---

law of liberty" (vs. 25) but do nothing about it. The ones who hear only and do not practice righteousness deceive themselves by making a false estimate of their standing before God. They may "enjoy" hearing the word preached, or they may read and think that they are serving the Lord; but in the void of their neglect of that word, their religion is vain.

[23] James' illustration presents in parable form the uselessness of being a mere listener to the word of God. The word is a kind of **mirror** in which we see our true selves and how far short we are from being and doing as we should. If looking into such a mirror does not lead to efforts to correct and improve ourselves, then we are like the man who looks into a common mirror and does not profit from it.

Observes often means to "look with contemplation or reflection" (Luke 12:27; cf. also 12:37; Acts 7:31f.; 11:6). The idea is not so much that he takes only a fleeting glance (as some commentators think) but that he looks and goes away and does not remember. The contrast is in the verb "perseveres" in verse 25.

His natural face is literally "the face of his birth" (see note on 3:6, "cycle of nature"), that is, the face or appearance which is his as a result of his physical birth. The corresponding image which we see in the mirror of God's word is our spiritual image or condition.

The ancients did not have mirrors made of glass and quicksilver. Theirs were of polished metal, such as alloys of tin or copper or of silver or gold, yet these were adequate for one to see himself.

[24] The illustration implies that the mirror revealed something that needed correcting. One goes to a mirror to see how he looks—if his hair needs combing or cutting, if his face needs washing, etc. When one sees himself, he sees his good and bad points.

Self-Examination — JAMES 1:24, 25

²⁵But he who looks into the perfect law, the law of liberty, and perseveres, being no hearer that forgets but a doer that acts, he shall be blessed in his doing.

James does not draw the full comparison. But he is thinking of the ethical condition of man in comparison to the demands laid out in the word of God. From our point of view one might think of the image of Jesus, which we are to imitate and into which we are to grow. This gives concreteness to the kind of character God wants us to be. Consider the Sermon on the Mount and look especially at the moral and ethical parts of the epistles in the New Testament. Here we get the picture of ourselves as God wants us to be. When we look, we see ourselves in relation to the will of God; and, as implied, we will see our defects or shortcomings, as well as our duty. Whether it does us good depends on whether we are like the man in James' parable.

[25] Some may profit from looking into the mirror, and some may profit from looking into the mirror of God's word. But only certain ones will—those described in this verse. The verb **looks** means to "bend over to look" and its usage indicates the meaning of "examine thoroughly or minutely." So angels who wonder about man's salvation "long to look into these things" (1 Peter 1:12; see also John 20:5, 11). The look at God's word must be more than a glance, if we see ourselves as God would see us.

The **perfect law** must be interpreted in the context as the same as the "word of truth" (vs. 18), the "implanted word" (vs. 21), and simply "the word" in verse 22, and possibly "the faith" (objective) of 2:1. James calls this "a law," and by all of this he must mean the body of truth or the word (message) which constitutes the foundation of the religion of Jesus Christ. This word was contained in the preaching of the apostles of Jesus and then was committed to written form to constitute what we know as the Christian Scriptures or the New Testament. In what sense this is to be considered a "law" is to be studied below. That he uses it to summarize or call attention to the teaching of the gospel is quite evident.

Why does James speak of this law or word as **perfect**? The gospel is the **perfect** law because it is a later and more perfect revelation than the law of Moses—a higher and more enlightening revelation of God's will than the former law. In fact, the Christian point of view is that it is the final and complete revelation of God's will (cf. Jude 3). The Christian expects no "latter-day revelation." Whatever may be the meaning of the term "law" in 4:11 (see on that verse), James nowhere contains a contrast of the word of truth with the law of Moses in terms of Peter (Acts 15:10) and Paul (in Gal., e.g., 5:4; 4:9; Rom. 7:2; Eph. 2:14; Col. 2:14). But there is nothing in James contradictory to this point of view, and James' view points in their direction, especially in our present passage and in 2:12. The New Testament writers see the gospel as the fulfillment and logical outcome of the Old Testament (Acts 24:14ff.; Rom. 13:8-10), especially in respect to the law's purpose and moral demands. The gospel achieves what the law tried but could not do (Rom. 8:3; Gal. 3:11; Heb. 7:19). But the gospel also is qualitatively better than the law. It reveals things previously not even imagined (2 Cor. 2:9-12; 1 Peter 1:10ff.). As the church is the better and more perfect tabernacle (Heb. 9:11), so the word of truth, as the law which is brought in through the changing of the law of Moses (Heb. 7:12), is **the perfect law.**

If James calls the word of truth a **law,** in what sense is this true? Paul once said that Christians are not under law but under grace (Rom. 6:14; see also John 1:17). Paul does not mean that we are not under *the* law (of Moses), but he means that the gospel is not a system of law, but of grace. If this is so, how then does James here (and indeed Paul himself in other places) refer to the gospel as a law (Gal. 6:2, "law of Christ"; Rom. 3:27, "principle of faith"; 8:2, "law of the Spirit")? The answer is found in the meaning of the qualifying phrases used with the term. Here in James it is to be found in the meaning of the term **law of liberty.**

The expression "law (or "principle") of faith" in Paul seems to mean a law which demands faith rather than works as the basis of merit; the "law of the Spirit" is the law which demands that the individual submit himself to the leadings of the Holy Spirit given by Christ and dwelling within him (Rom. 8:2). The "law of Christ" in Galatians 6:2 seems to mean Christ's "new commandment" (John 13:34), the "law of love" (which is, of course, the same as James' "royal law" in 2:8); this is the "old commandment which you had from the beginning" which is yet new (1 John 2:7ff.). The term **law of liberty** (which is actually a paradox, for law in its nature is restraint or limitation rather than freedom) means "freedom" or **liberty** in Christ as a principle of life.

One understands the gospel of Christ only when he understands this paradox. Failure to understand it leads either to legalism or to antinomianism (unrestrained excess). Paul in Galatians 5:1 declares that Christ has set us free; however, we must not consider this as license (Gal. 5:13). Christians are to put themselves under a law of love to become *slaves* (this is the literal meaning of "servants" in the passage) to one another (5:13). This is as if a slave freed legally by his master wanted to continue as a slave (of his own choice or liberty) because of the great love which he had for his master. The word of Christ is a law in the sense that it is a revelation of Christ's will or desire for us; it is his commandment. Obedience is the "obedience of faith," rendered freely out of gratitude or love to God and Christ for their grace (Rom. 16:26). Thus as to the "word of truth" as a system of salvation, "we are not under law"; but, when the word is considered a test of faith and love to him, we are "under the law of Christ" (1 Cor. 9:21). This paradoxical way of speaking is the very essence of Christianity. If one sees the "duties" of the teaching of Christ or his apostles as a check list of obligations which he obeys and thus earns his salvation as a matter of "obedience," he is a legalist without real understanding of the gospel of Christ. But if one thinks that, being freed from law, he can follow his own inclinations in the teaching and practice of the truth, he is considered a reprobate and a heretic (Titus 1:15, 16; 3:10, etc.).

James himself shows that the **law of liberty** does not mean that the Christian is free from regulation. If he shows partiality and is without pity for the poor, he sins (2:9) and will be judged without mercy (2:13). If he errs as a teacher, he will be judged with greater strictness (3:1). If he is worldly, he becomes God's enemy (4:4) and a sinner (4:8). If he swears, he falls under condemnation (5:12). Or if he wanders from the truth, he may die (the second death) (5:20).

What a wonderful system Jesus gave to us by his death! "God's love has been poured into our hearts through the Holy Spirit which has been given to us. While we were still weak, at the right time Christ died for the ungodly" (Rom. 5:5f.). If we would serve God from such motivation, what a difference there would be in our worship and service. Who could consider any "duty" placed upon him by such a Savior a burden? Who would have the effrontery to inject his will or "think so" into his service against the will of such a Lord?

The hearer who responds by doing, after looking into the **law of liberty,** will be blessed.

The verb used by James for **perseveres** is used by Paul in Philippians 1:25 of his continuing to live in the midst of the churches. But it is John who gave the word its distinctive meaning in the New Testament, as he used it to emphasize the continuing to live by or abiding in the word (John 8:31; 2 John 9). And see 1 Timothy 2:15; 2 Timothy 3:14. James' point is not far different, for he implies that action must follow the continuing to look.

A hearer that forgets and a **doer that acts** are literally "a hearer of forgetfulness" and a "doer of work." They mean "not a forgetful hearer" but an "active worker." Consider such parallels as "steward of dishonesty" for "dishonest steward" (Luke 16:8) and "judges with evil thoughts" for "evil-thinking judges" in James 2:4.

Being **blessed in his doing** is the approbation and reward of God for a "well done." Compare the words of Jesus in John 13:17. In Jesus' parable of the wise and unwise builders (Matt. 7:24ff.) the blessing is that of having the house to stand. The blessing is in the doing; it is realized in the continuous application to duty in a free spirit.

The Application: Pure and Vain Religion, 1:26, 27

James now selects three things which illustrate how a man may be a hearer of the word—how he may, in fact, be very

External Religion JAMES 1:26

²⁶If any one thinks he is religious, and does not bridle his tongue but deceives his heart, this man's religion is vain.

attendant upon the "services" of the church—and still be a "forgetful hearer" whose religion is vain. The three are control of the tongue, benevolence, and purity of life.

[26] The verb **thinks** means to "fancy or suppose." James is speaking of the man who deceives himself, not an insincere person (1 Cor. 3:18). A man may suppose himself to be devout or pious while not heeding what he has heard about self-control of the tongue. Another possible meaning is "has a reputation as" (cf. Gal. 2:2, 6; Mark 10:42). But the use of the word **deceives** seems to favor the other meaning.

The word **religious** carries the idea of "external rite" or "service" (cf. Acts 26:5; Col. 2:18). Many people "go to services," and this is a scriptural idea as here. Formal worship is "service" or devotion to God. Though a similar verb is used in the Jewish book of Sirach (11:15; 14:16) in the sense of superstition and worship of false gods, the use of verse 27 ("pure and undefiled" religion) forbids that meaning here. The meaning is that one may be a worshiper of God in vain. The warning is in line with the Old Testament prophets who emphasized that the service of God in sacrifices and sabbath keeping or tithing was of no value if one disregarded the duty of justice and mercy and faith. A church or a member of the church can have a name that he lives and be dead (Rev. 3:1) or think himself rich when he is poor (3:17).

The thought in **bridle his tongue** is a revival of the idea "quick to hear, slow to speak" in verse 19, and it is, of course, expounded more at length in chapter 3 where the cognate noun for "bridle" is also used for illustrating control of the tongue. The idea is to restrain, control, and guide the tongue or speech in the proper direction. This is a prime consideration of Bible teaching in both Old and New Testaments: Psalm 39:1; Job 2:10; Matthew 12:34-37; 15:19; Ephesians 4:25-29.

The implied completion of the condition is "If any one thinks he is religious . . ." while he lacks self-control, then his religion is vain. See on verse 22, "deceiving yourselves." It

JAMES 1:27 — *Pure Religion*

²⁷Religion that is pure and undefiled before God and the Father is this: to visit orphans and widows in their affliction, and to keep oneself unstained from the world.

---

is useless for one to worship God who obviously omits such a vital part of what the true religion given by God is. Jesus taught that we should leave our gift at the altar and be reconciled to our brother before our worship is acceptable (Matt. 5:23). **Vain** means "useless," "empty," or "fruitless." So faith may be useless (1 Cor. 15:17; cf. also Titus 3:9; 1 Cor. 3:20; Matt. 15:8; and 1 Peter 1:18).

[27] Religion that is pure is the antithesis of the vain or empty religion just mentioned. We might expect "useful" as the antithesis, but James varies the parallel. **Pure** means "what is free from stain or sin" (as in "pure in heart," Matt. 5:8, and "clear conscience," 1 Tim. 3:9). If one holds the faith in partiality, he sins (2:9). So if one is indifferent to the suffering and is immoral in life, he sins. Only **pure** religion is useful. There seems to be no difference in **pure** and **undefiled**. Acceptable worship is that which combines religious service and a holy life with active participation in good deeds (see on James 3:17).

The standard of judgment of what is acceptable is God's, not ours. His is the only absolute standard of acceptability; we must do what is "good and acceptable in the sight of God" (1 Tim. 2:3). See Romans 2:13; Job 9:2; 1 Corinthians 3:19; Galatians 3:11; 2 Thessalonians 1:6; 1 Peter 2:4; 2 Peter 3:8.

Father seems to be added to emphasize that the God we worship is the Father. This emphasizes the aspect of his nature as love. If we worship God, who is father and who loves his creatures, while we ourselves are heartless and merciless, we ourselves should be able to see that there is something incongruous in our worship.

James defines the contents of pure religion in the following infinitives in both a positive and negative way. Of course this is not an exhaustive definition. James is merely illustrating. Later in the epistle James mentions other things which are a part of or a defect in service to God.

Visit Orphans and Widows   JAMES 1:27

To visit literally means "to look in on" or "go to see." But religiously the word had a long history in the sense of "supplying the needs of" or "caring for" (as in Jer. 23:2; Zech. 11:16; Matt. 25:36, 43). The meaning is especially fixed here by the term **affliction** or "distress," that is, their being destitute and hence lacking in the necessities of life. In the Old Testament the word is used of God's visiting his people by delivering them and supplying their needs and wishes (Gen. 21:1; Ex. 3:16; 4:31). Though the verb is cognate with the verb "to oversee" in the New Testament, this is not the meaning here (as has just been demonstrated by an examination of the context), and the verb does not mean here "to take them under the oversight of the church," that is, for the church itself to provide institutional care for the widows and orphans. But this does not preclude that elders are to take the lead in visiting and seeing that the wants of the needy are supplied. So Polycarp, an early Christian, wrote that elders "are to be tender-hearted, merciful to all, converting the erring, *visiting* all who are sick; not neglecting the *widow* or *orphan* or needy, and providing always what is good in the sight of God" (*Philippians* 6).

Orphans, that is, those "deprived (of their parents)," may occur either through death or abandonment. A **widow** is one who has been deprived of a husband in either of the above ways. (The word is derived from *charomai*, "I need.") The abandonment of a child (exposure), which was one of the common dark crimes of the ancient pagan world, resulted in many **orphans.** There is abundant evidence that neither word necessitates loss by death only.

The duty mentioned here is highlighted in the ministry of the early church. In Acts 6 daily ministrations to **widows** is put under the Seven; 1 Timothy 5:3 enjoins the support of **widows** who do not have relatives to support them. Old Testament references are numerous: Deuteronomy 26:19; Exodus 22:22; Job 31:16f.

The New Testament puts no limitation upon which **widows** or **orphans** are to be helped. Paul's rule is "Do good to all men, especially to those who are of the household of faith" (Gal. 6:10). One would assume that James' rule would work

> ¹**My brethren, show no partiality as you hold the faith of our Lord Jesus Christ, the Lord of glory.**

in the same way. Nor does the New Testament legislate on how such benevolence is to be administered.

The idea in **unstained** is that one should guard himself from the world of evil or corruption so that he is not defiled by it (cf. 1 Tim. 6:14; 1 Peter 1:19; 2 Peter 3:14). See in greater detail the comment on James 4:1-10. The **world** here is the realm of Satan, the world of evil men who are in the kingdom of evil (1 John 2:15). "Friendship with the world is enmity with God" (James 4:4). One must not defile himself with the sinful pleasures of the world if his worship is to be acceptable.

THE SIN OF RESPECT OF PERSONS, 2:1-13

Partiality in the Assembly, 2:1-4

The second chapter of James begins with a warning against the sin of partiality or respect of persons. It grows out of a sin which James seemingly knew to be prevalent among the Jewish churches and is related to his previous discussion by furnishing a further example of inconsistency on the part of those whose practice of pure and undefiled religion was defective. Just as those who were hearers and not doers lacked self-control over their tongues and did not exhibit the love that led to visiting the fatherless and widows, so also they showed that they did not possess the right attitude toward poor people. James rebukes them sharply and calls them "evil" and "sinners." The thought of James 1:26f. that religion must reflect the great importance of conduct is now enlarged in a specific illustration of something of which many of his readers were guilty.

[1] My brethren, James' oft-repeated address, seems very appropriate here, where he takes up a breach of brotherly love.

Hold (the faith) is a characteristic Greek expression for possessing a trait or inner quality. It occurs in such expressions as "have love" (John 5:42) and "have hope" (Acts

24:15). Other occurrences are Acts 14:9; Romans 14:22; 1 Timothy 1:19. It means virtually the same as to "believe in" something. Thus **faith** is subjective and does not refer to the teaching or doctrine to be received (as in Gal. 1:23). This indicates also that **of the Lord Jesus Christ** is objective and means "have faith in" or "believe in" the Lord Jesus Christ. For this usage see Romans 3:26; Galatians 2:16; Ephesians 3:12; Philippians 3:9. Having such faith is an essential element of being a Christian. "To have faith" in such a context is virtually the same as "to be a Christian." "The believers" or simply "believing" is often a simple way of saying "Christians."

Jesus is described either as **the Lord of glory** or as "the Lord, the glory" (apposition). The arrangement of the words makes it difficult to decide; both yield good sense. The first expression means either that he is the Lord of the realm of glory or brightness, where God lives, or it is a qualitative (descriptive) modifier meaning "the glorious Lord." If it is to be taken as an appositive with **the Lord Jesus Christ,** it means Jesus "who is the glory." The thought is that of the identification of Jesus (or the transference to him) with the Shekinah or "glory" of God by which his presence was signified at the tabernacle in the Old Testament. See Exodus 24:17; 40:34; Numbers 14:10.

Some things are incompatible with faith in Jesus Christ. John taught that one could not love God and hate his brother (1 John 4:20). Faith in Jesus as Lord excludes **partiality** or respect of persons. To hold Jesus in proper respect as Lord necessitates the right attitude toward men. So James demands that Christians quit combining faith in Jesus with the wrong attitude toward the poor.

Partiality in the Greek originally meant to "lift up the face of someone" or to "receive him with favor." So in Malachi 1:8, "Will he be pleased with you or show you favor?" It then came to mean "show favoritism" (see Lev. 19:15; Ps. 82:2). The noun itself is not used in the Septuagint, but its meaning is clear. It is found in Romans 2:11; Ephesians 6:9; and Colossians 3:25. One of the laws in the Old Testament was: "You shall do no injustice in judgment;

²For if a man with gold rings and in fine clothing comes into your assembly, and a poor man in shabby clothing also comes in,

---

you shall not be partial to the poor or defer to the great, but in righteousness shall you judge your neighbor" (Lev. 19:15). The Pharisees and chief priests flattered Jesus that "he did not receive persons," i.e., "show not favor" (Goodspeed) or "pay no deference" (NEB). It is distinctly noted in the New Testament that God shows no partiality (Acts 10:34). For this reason, masters must not threaten (Eph. 6:9); slaves must not do wrong (Col. 3:25). God does not even favor those reputed to be something (Gal. 2:6). He will judge impartially (Rom. 2:11; 1 Peter 1:17). Using another word of the same meaning, Paul tells Timothy that he is to treat elders impartially (1 Tim. 5:21). Thus the importance of the principle is seen. In the context the evil judging of people by appearances or partiality is called "evil thinking," "sin," and "transgression."

James is dealing with the sin of showing **partiality** because of wealth. In our age it might be the same, or it might be social standing, occupation, nationality, or color. James would insist that distinctions of persons in the church are sins.

[2] James dramatizes the sin of partiality by a concrete example: action in the very **assembly.** The Greek is literally "synagogue," which was the technical term for a Jewish congregation or group meeting for worship (Matt. 4:23; Acts 17:1). It was also used by metonomy for the place of meeting (Luke 7:5). The literal meaning of the word, however, had no religious connotation. Compare its use in Genesis 1:9 for the gatherings of water. It means literally a "bringing together" or "assemblying" (from *sun,* "together," and *agō,* "I lead or bring"). The use here to describe an assembly of Christians is probably to be seen as a reflection of the situation where the churches (especially the Jewish churches) are still so closely related to the synagogues of the Jews that no great distinction is made between them. Notice how Paul separated the disciples from the synagogue (Acts 19:9). The Jewish Christians

Fine Clothing — JAMES 2:2, 3

³**and you pay attention to the one who wears the fine clothing and say, "Have a seat here, please," while you say to the poor man, "Stand there," or, "Sit at my feet,"**

would probably continue for some time to call their own assemblies after their Jewish names. It is certain that the synagogue influenced the early churches a great deal. The organization of the local churches with a plurality of elders seems to have been taken over from the synagogue. So it is not surprising that James still uses the term. An inscription of the early fourth century A.D. is mentioned in Arndt-Gingrich bearing the reading "synagogue of the Marcionites" from near Damascus.

One can almost see the picture of the congregation meeting together in some rented hall or some house belonging to a member and the two strangers (certainly outsiders) entering (not necessarily at the same time). It is implied that they are strangers, for the treatment accorded each is based upon looks, not upon previous knowledge of their characters. The first visitor is a rich man, who comes probably out of curiosity. His **gold rings** (Luke 15:22) and **fine clothing** indicate that he is rich. The sources show that the wearing of rings was a custom. Often rings were worn on all but the middle finger. So bad did the ostentation become that some early Christian writers thought that Christians should avoid rings altogether except for sealing documents. **Fine clothing** is literally "bright" or "shining" apparel. Luke uses the same expression for the clothing of the angel who appeared to Peter (Acts 10:30) and for the clothes Herod put on Jesus in mockery (Luke 23:11). The rich man is followed by a **poor man** in **shabby** clothes. James is even more specific; the words literally describe his dress as "dirty" or "filthy" (cf. the figurative use of the word for moral uncleanness in Rev. 22:11).

[3] The verb **pay attention to** means "take a look at" (Luke 9:38) or "fix the eyes upon." Then it means to "gaze fixedly on" or "pay special attention to" (NEB). In Luke 1:48 it has a sense of "care especially for." Here the verb calls attention to the fixing of the eyes of the people on the visitor,

JAMES 2:3, 4 — *Distinctions*

⁴have you not made distinctions among yourselves, and become judges with evil thoughts?

---

then to the special attention paid to him as the impression is created by his dress that he is "somebody." There is some discussion as to whether the word rendered **please** really means this or rather "in a good place." At any rate, the suggestion is that of a cordial reception. Our sources mention the custom of designating seats in assemblies: Luke 11:43; 20:46; Mark 12:39.

Letting a visitor **stand** rather than providing a seat (even if some member has to stand) is a mark of discourtesy among most people. To have to **sit** on the floor at someone's feet is equally a slight, unless it is that of voluntary submission of the student to his teacher, as in Luke 8:35; 10:39 (of Martha at Jesus' feet); and Acts 22:3. The incident which James has recreated is probably just a typical way in which the respect of persons was shown. There may have been other ways (cf. 1 Cor. 11:22).

[4] The verb **made distinctions** has the double sense of making distinctions and of doubting or wavering. This accounts for the margin of the ASV "Are ye not divided in your own mind?" Oesterley takes the verb in the latter sense as indicating a spirit of class distinctions among them which would divide the church, a meaning which is in Josephus (*Wars* I. 27); *4 Maccabees* 1:14; and in the New Testament in Acts 15:9 ("made no distinction between us and them"); and 1 Corinthians 4:7 ("who sees anything different in you?"). Compare also Acts 11:12, "Go with them, making no distinction." Mayor is similar but suggests the idea is that of inner divisions, the double mind of 1:8. This means that there is a sharp distinction between what one thinks at one time (profession) and what one thinks or does at another (practice). This is, then, a form of "wavering, doubting, or hesitating." This meaning for the verb seems to have been used first in the New Testament. Goodspeed translates "waver." Either meaning of the verb is well attested and will fit the context. The meaning "make distinction" seems to fit better; at least it goes better with the next word **become judges.** At any rate,

Judging

the idea of James is that their actions represent a vacillation, either of a group among its members or of individuals in consistency or inner approval of a course of action. The end result is judging the worth of men by appearances.

The Greek has literally "judges of evil thoughts." The possessive is a descriptive or qualitative use (as in 1:25, "hearer of forgetfulness" = "forgetful hearer") and is equal to "evil-thinking judges." Mayor translates "wrong-considering judges." In 4:11 James says that the one who speaks against his neighbor judges him. Jesus said that evil judging rises from the heart (Matt. 15:19) and is one of the things which defile the man. In making distinctions on outward appearances they were judging. Jesus had judging from appearances in mind when he said, "Judge not that you be not judged" (Matt. 7:1). Only God is qualified to judge; even when we see evidence of evil deeds, human judgments are not correct, because we cannot know the heart. Judgments on the basis of the kind of clothing worn is even less judicious and hence **evil** or sinful.

God's Judgments, 2:5-13

The argument of verses 5-13 runs as follows: God judges by different standards from those being used by James' readers. He has selected as his own the poor of the world, for as a group they possess the faith to be heirs of the kingdom. The rich, on the other hand, oppress the poor and blaspheme the name called upon the Christians. It is assumed that some claim that in their action they were fulfilling the royal law given by Moses to love the neighbor. If this is so, it is well so far as it goes. But the principle of justifying ourselves by the law demands that every law be kept. It takes only the breaking of one law to make a lawbreaker. The same law that teaches to love one's neighbor teaches also not to respect persons. So the appeal to the law fails as long as partiality is shown.

All the Christian's acts are to be judged, as James had already shown, by the law of liberty. This law actually frees him from the law as such and judges him by the law of love. Such a law implies mercy and procures for the one showing

> **⁵Listen, my beloved brethren. Has not God chosen those who are poor in the world to be rich in faith and heirs of the kingdom which he has promised to those who love him?**

mercy the mercy of God himself. So the one who speaks and acts as one to be judged in this way may be happy and confident in the face of impending judgment.

[5] This verse sets forth the proof that the action of the readers is wrong. Their favoritism is both inconsistent with God's attitude toward the poor and also with the attitude of the rich themselves toward God's people. The Jew was confident that he was God's chosen (Deut. 14:1, 2). Back of the thought is the idea that it was not any intrinsic merit or wealth that caused the selection, but the promise of Israel's fulfilling God's purpose in their faith. The New Testament adopts this as fulfilled in the church. Christians are God's elect (Eph. 1:4; 1 Peter 1:1). A lack of worldly pride is seen in the fulfillment: "But God chose what is foolish in the world to shame the wise; God chose what is weak in the world to shame the strong" (1 Cor. 1:27). This same concept lies behind James' words. God has **chosen those who are poor** in some respects (i.e., in regard to the world) but **rich** in another (i.e., in regard to the faith) to be his own and to be the **heirs** of his promises. This does not mean **rich in faith** as though they had faith in abundance, nor does it mean that their faith is their riches. The dative is the dative of relationship, like "beautiful before God" in Acts 7:20 and "powerful in respect to God" in 2 Corinthians 10:4. The wealth that is connected with the faith of the Christian is the same as that to which he is heir—the kingdom, the salvation which is in Christ.

Whether the RSV is right in taking **rich in faith,** etc., to be an implied predicate (supplying **to be** rich) is open to question. What the language says as it stands is that God chose the poor, rich in faith, and heirs of the kingdom. These are the kind he chooses. When one becomes these, he is one of the chosen. This does not make the poor as a class destined to become rich in faith and heirs, nor does it exclude the rich. It merely observes that there is a condescension in God's choice. Poverty and election usually coincide. God knew that

The Poor Man — JAMES 2:5, 6

⁶But you have dishonored the poor man. Is it not the rich who oppress you, is it not they who drag you into court?

---

the world would be so constituted that those fulfilling his purpose would largely fall among this group, and so it has happened (1 Cor. 1:26). The rich themselves may qualify, as James has indicated in 1:10. (See also 1 Tim. 6:17ff.) But riches are a danger for one and make his way to salvation difficult (Matt. 19:23ff.).

James' point is quite plain: Of the two visitors to the service, the poor is much more likely to become a Christian and become an heir of the heavenly kingdom; yet the Christians so look upon worldly appearances that they favor the other man. It is not that they ought to be discourteous to either person; but they should not dishonor either, especially the poor. In mistreating the poor they are mistreating the same kind of people as themselves.

From this James turns to the way the rich generally treat the Christians.

[6] The action of the church in showing partiality and giving the rich man the good seat and making the poor stand or sit on the floor simply because of his poverty had "dishonored this poor man." "Despised" is a possible meaning, but by etymology and usage the word usually meant to **dishonor** or "show disrespect to." The verb usually means "to insult or degrade" (Mark 12:4; Acts 5:41). "The poor man" is the generic use of the singular noun with the article, not merely "this poor man," but the poor as such. See James 5:6 for what is probably a similar usage.

The verb **oppress** means to "dominate" or "exercise power over," almost always in a bad sense. It is at times used of the tyrannical rule of the devil or evil spirits over men (Acts 10:38). It signifies also exploiting people, often being used in the Old Testament of exploiting widows and orphans (Micah 2:2; Amos 8:4; Zech. 7:10; and Jer. 7:6).

The very people being honored are guilty of dragging or having Christians dragged into court. James is probably thinking of the rich Sadducees who persecuted Christians (Acts 4:1; 13:50). The Sadducees, though small in number,

⁷Is it not they who blaspheme the honorable name which was invoked over you?

controlled the Sanhedrin with its wealth acquired from the tribute money from Jews all over the world. They were the chief instigators of the early persecutions of the church. Christians because they were despised may also have been often singled out by the rich merchants and landowners and prosecuted for their debts. **Drag** implies force and is actually mentioned in cases of arrest in Acts 9:1; 16:19; 21:30. Such is the kind of action Jesus had forewarned his disciples about (Matt. 10:7; John 16:2). Local Jewish **courts** were permitted by the Romans (Matt. 10:17; 9:2; 26:11; 1 Cor. 6:2, 4).

[7] To **blaspheme** is to "revile" or "speak disrespectfully" of something that is honorable or sacred. The word is usually translated "blaspheme" when it is something holy or sacred (Acts 19:37; Rom. 2:24), but literally the word means to "speak evil" (Titus 3:2; Rom. 3:8).

The **name** meant is undoubtedly (in view of biblical usage) the name of Jesus. The Jews would not ordinarily blaspheme the name Christ (Messiah), which was a title sacred to them, except as they might do so by ironically ridiculing the claim of Jesus to be the Christ (as in Mark 15:32). **Blaspheme** here implies the desecration of the name in the knowledge that Christians considered it a worthy or sacred name. First Corinthians 12:3 ("Jesus be cursed") shows that some cursed the name of Jesus. Zahn and others think the reference is to rich Christians who apostatize and in persecution curse the name of Jesus as Lord, the idea being that the rich were more easily induced to do this. This Plummer and Mayor reject, pointing out that "over you" (rather than "upon them") differentiates the readers from those who do this. Luke speaks of the unbelieving Jews (Acts 13:45) literally as "contradicting, speaking blasphemy."

The passive (as in the ASV margin) is properly to be read: "which is called upon you." The background for the phrase is Amos 9:12, quoted in Acts 15:17: "I will build again the tabernacle of David . . . that the rest of men may seek the Lord, and all the Gentiles," upon whom my name is

⁸If you really fulfil the royal law, according to the scripture, "You shall love your neighbor as yourself," you do well.

called. The passive of the verb here is used with the noun "name" as in the Old Testament to designate the object as the property of the one wearing the name. See 2 Samuel 6:2 (of the ark); 1 Kings 8:43; Jeremiah 7:30 (of the temple); Jeremiah 14:9 (of Israel); and also Numbers 6:27; 2 Chronicles 7:14; Isaiah 63:19; Jeremiah 25:29. It is even used of the wife assuming the husband's name (Isa. 4:1) and of the children (Gen. 48:16). Actually it makes little difference whether the active or passive translation is given, since, after the name is invoked over one, it is assumed by him and he is called by it (Isa. 43:7). This does not mean that the Israelite wore a form of Jehovah's name; it was fulfilled in his acknowledging that he belonged to Jehovah. So James had said, "James, a servant of God and of the Lord Jesus Christ" (1:1). This is the meaning of the NEB translation: "The honored name by which God has claimed you," which gives the significance of the wording rather than the translation.

In view of this background the probability is that the reference is to the invocation of the name of Jesus Christ upon the believer at baptism (Acts 2:38, "in the name of Jesus Christ"; and see 8:16; 10:48). "Calling on the name of Jesus" (Acts 22:16) is different. This signifies calling upon God or Jesus (cf. 1 Sam. 12:17f.) or their name (Gen. 13:4; 21:33) in worship (prayer). This may be in a plea for help (2 Sam. 22:7) in recognition of authority (as is probably Acts 3:6; 19:13). Stephen died "calling upon the name of the Lord" (Acts 7:59); his actual words were "Lord Jesus, receive my spirit." The concept occurs often: Acts 2:21; 9:14; Romans 10:13f.; 1 Corinthians 1:2; and especially 2 Timothy 2:22.

From this it is very unlikely that the reference is to the derogatory use of the name "Christian."

[8] This section has some difficulties of interpretation, but the sense seems to be as follows: James anticipates that some of his hearers will justify their showing favors to the

JAMES 2:8, 9 — *Royal Law*

9But if you show partiality, you commit sin, and are convicted by the law as transgressors.

rich by referring to the commandment which said that the Jew was to love his neighbor as himself. It may be that James knew that this was already being used as an excuse. He shows that such an attempt fails as a justification of the action on the grounds that it falls short of fulfilling the whole law.

The royal law is identified by James as summed up in (**according to**) loving one's neighbor (Lev. 19:18). Why is this called the **royal** law? It is either because of its transcending importance among the laws of the Old Testament (cf. Jesus' saying that this was the "second" like "Love the Lord your God with all your heart") or because it is from the king (compare "royal country" = "the king's country," Acts 12:20). At any rate, the appeal is to the law of love as that of first importance. James' critics are saying, "Surely an action which fulfils such a law could not be wrong."

James has no quarrel with fulfilling the righteousness of the law. Nor does the New Testament ever have. What was morally right under the law is an expression of God's will and is the object of achievement under the gospel (Rom. 7; 8:3; 13:10). There is little difference between the morality of the law and the gospel, though there is a difference in application. If one actually was trying to fulfill the concept of love as laid down in the law, he would be doing excellently.

[9] James assumed that **partiality** was present among them, just as he had assumed that they were attempting to fulfil the royal law. (In both places he used a condition assumed as fulfilled.) The partiality had been demonstrated in the favor to the rich. The excuse involved the readers in an inconsistency which James goes on to explain. **You commit sin** means (compare note on 1:20) "You practice sin," become guilty of sinning. The reason that this can be said so specifically is that the law plainly forbade this. Partiality was prohibited in the same chapter which speaks of love of neighbor, Leviticus 19:15: "You shall do no injustice in judgment: you shall not be partial to the poor, or defer to the great." (Cf. Deut. 1:17; 16:19.) Thus the law points to the one who

Guilty of All JAMES 2:10, 11

¹⁰For whoever keeps the whole law but fails in one point has become guilty of all of it. ¹¹For he who said, "Do not commit adultery," said also, "Do not kill." If you do not commit adultery but do kill, you have become a transgressor of the law.

---

respects persons as a transgressor. By an appeal to the law, nothing but sin can be made of their action toward the poor.

[10] This verse is difficult, but it is usually interpreted as follows. It states the principle which makes the former argument valid. The keeping of the whole law is useless as a matter of justification unless it is kept perfectly.

The verb **fail** here, as in James 3:2, means to "sin" (see Rom. 11:11; 2 Peter 1:10; Jude 24). **In one point** means "one precept or commandment" with the word **point** understood.

Become guilty of all of it means to become guilty of violating the law as a whole—of becoming a lawbreaker. One does not need to go to rabbinical parallels to illustrate this. Paul stated the principle to the Galatians: "Cursed be every one who does not abide by all things written in the book of the law, and do them" (Gal. 3:10). Nor is this a strange rule even in civil law. If one murders, he becomes a lawbreaker and may pay the supreme penalty, though he may have kept all law for many years. Paul explains in Romans 7 that the law of sin in our members brings us into sin even if we desire to keep the law. So we all sin (cf. James 3:2). This is the reason that one cannot be justified by the law; he cannot keep it perfectly as he must do to be declared innocent (be justified).

Thus James is saying that those who appeal to the law to justify their partiality are condemned as transgressors because they are guilty of breaking another precept in the same action. James is not saying that the law is still binding upon Christians as such; he is answering those who appeal to the law of love to justify their sin. This is clear from verse 12. Christians are under the law of love. Under this they are really free from the *law* to love their neighbor (Gal. 5:13) but have become slaves to Christ and their neighbors *out of love*.

[11] Commentators labor explaining why James chooses these two commands (perhaps because they offend most

¹²So speak and so act as those who are to be judged under the law of liberty.

against the law of love?). These are likely chosen as typical laws. The law is an expression of the will of the lawgiver. One cannot pick out the law which pleases him and let the others go. The only way to be approved by the law is to keep the whole law.

Paul in Romans 2 pointed out the inconsistency of the Jews, who took pride in themselves as "teachers" or "guides to the blind": they only taught the law but did not keep it, or they kept one part and neglected the other (Rom. 2:17ff.).

So if one keeps some laws but breaks others, he has **become a transgressor of the law.** Thus by the appeal for a judgment by the law, those showing partiality condemn themselves as sinners.

[12] James uses imperatives in the present tense for continuous action. We are to live continuously both in our words and speech in view of the way we are to be judged.

Jesus emphasized the urgency of the Christian life. The Christian expects the Lord at any time. He must be ready at any time to give account. At the time when the world expects not, the Lord will come. The construction used in Greek **(who are to be judged)** refers to things sure to come to pass. It was a favorite construction in expressing decrees or what was fixed by necessity (Matt. 25:31; 2 Cor. 5:10; Acts 11:28; 24:25; 27:10). **Judged** here does not mean, as in some other passages in James, "condemned" (cf. 4:11), but it means to be confronted by the judge to be assessed as guilty or justified according to law. Christians understand that they are to be judged by the gospel of Jesus Christ (Rom. 2:16).

The **law of liberty** is a reference to the description of the "word of truth" or the "implanted word" (1:18, 21), as "the law of liberty" in James 1:25. For the meaning of the expression, see the comment on that passage. It seems most likely that James repeats his reference to this term by way of contrast with the law or test being proposed by those who were guilty of partiality. They had implied that they justified their action by appealing to the royal law of Leviticus 19:18. James

Judgment — JAMES 2:12, 13

¹³For judgment is without mercy to one who has shown no mercy; yet mercy triumphs over judgment.

---

has countered by showing that that provision is a part of the whole of the Jewish law, which included the Ten Commandments. Justification under that law demands a consistency of action in keeping the whole law; one cannot just choose which he would keep and let the others go. Partiality is condemned by the same law, so no appeal to the law can be made to justify something it condemns. Having shown that this device will not work, James then in our present verse says, in effect, that Christians are not judged by the law of Moses anyway, but by the perfect law, the law of liberty. Remembering the free yoke which we have assumed to the will of Christ, out of the gratitude which we owe to him, we ought to act toward the poor as that law of love (freely assumed and no longer a burden of law) indicates that we should. The exact stipulation of that law, of course, is that we are all one man in Christ Jesus: whether Jew or Greek, bond or free, rich or poor. Our judgment as Christians will not be as a matter of law but as a matter of obedience to this law of liberty.

[13] The **judgment** referred to is that implicit in the expression of the previous verse "judged under the law of liberty." The judgment which Christians will be subjected to is that of the gospel of Christ. Christ's teaching about that judgment shows plainly what basis will be used to justify his followers, those "blessed of the Father" who will be welcomed into the "joys of the Lord." But those who have not ministered to the unfortunate will be told, "Depart from me, you cursed" (Matt. 25:41). Even under the law of liberty no mercy will be shown those who do not meet the test of mercy to others.

Mercy in such an expression as this is virtually a synonym for the right attitude toward the poor. "Pity" or "compassion" on those without the necessities of life (the widow, the fatherless, the one without food and clothing), as in 1:27, is a vital part of Christ's law of love. This teaching is quite plain. This Jesus illustrated in the parable of the unmerciful servant (Matt. 18:23-35). The principle of reciprocity is basic to forgiveness. He who is not forgiving cannot be forgiven. But the classic expression is Jesus' own picture of the last judgment, in which the disciples are separated as the shepherd separates the sheep from the goats on the basis of whether "you did it to one of the least of these my brethren" (Matt. 25:31-46). John asks how one could claim that the love of God dwells in him who sees a brother hungry and does not feed him (1 John 3:17). Love must be not merely in word but in deed. This is James' climax to the discussion of the sin of judging. Those who take the attitude of despising the poor, as they were doing, will face the judgment under the law of liberty **without mercy,** for they have **shown no mercy** to the poor.

Mercy triumphs over judgment states the opposite and favorable side: Those who have shown mercy under the law of liberty may face that judgment with confidence. Mercy "glories" or "boasts" against the threat of judgment because it leaves the judgment with nothing to condemn. The man who has loved the poor and has shown mercy toward them (all other things being equal) will be justified in the last judgment and will receive the blessing of Christ. Just as "love casts out fear" (1 John 4:18), so having mercy relieves the Christian of the fear of judgment.

Thus James deals with the sin of partiality in the church. He has shown that it is clearly inconsistent with the Christian's profession of faith in the Lord Jesus Christ.

THE RELATION OF FAITH AND WORKS, 2:14-26

The last half of James 2 constitutes one of the best known and most controversial sections of the epistle—indeed, of the whole Bible. Martin Luther thought that James here was in direct opposition to Paul's teaching on justification by faith in Romans; and, since he considered Paul's doctrine as the touchstone for interpreting the New Testament, he considered James an inferior part of the canon—a "right strawy epistle." At the proper point the relationship of James and Paul in their teaching on justification will be examined.

James and Paul

The relation of this section to the earlier parts of the letter should not be lost sight of. James has insisted that true religion must show itself in proper response. It is not merely the hearer who is saved by the word, but the doer. Religious works or acts of service which do not find accompaniment in works of love and moral living are vain (James 1:22-25). Faith toward Christ must not be held with respect of persons, or the Christian becomes a sinner (James 2:1-8). James now shows that faith as the foundation attitude of the gospel must find expression in works of obedience if it is to be a saving or justifying faith. If it does not, it is a dead faith; and the man who thinks that such faith will save is mistaken. There must be more than faith; works must help faith for it to achieve its purpose of justification. But one will not understand James 2:14-26 unless it is remembered that with James, no less than with Paul, faith is the necessary foundation or ground of salvation.

Some have wondered if James was refuting Paul's language in Romans 3-4. This can hardly be true if one accepts both letters as inspired. The Spirit of God does not refute itself. It is quite possible to demonstrate that there is no necessary contradiction between the meaning and application of the two passages. Others think that James may have been correcting a wrong use of Paul's teaching by some of the early Christians. This is only barely possible. Paul wrote the Roman letter in the year A.D. 58 and James died in the early 60s. We do know, of course, that some of Paul's teaching was abused, such as his teaching of grace, which was used to teach antinomianism (Rom. 6:1ff.). Thus some may have excused their lack of obedience to the law of liberty by seizing upon Paul's teaching that justification was by faith as the merit apart from the works of the law.

Other commentators, however, feel that it is unlikely that Palestinian Jewish Christians would have appropriated and misused Paul's doctrine. They feel that James is simply writing against the tendency of Jews to feel that their racial and religious position with superior knowledge and beliefs put them in a more favorable position with God and, in fact, guaranteed them salvation even without adequate response to the teaching. This was the shallowness which had been refuted by the great prophets of the Old Testament. There would still be such pride and shallowness in some Jews who were attracted to or embraced Christianity. Nicodemus thought that by accepting Jesus as a teacher come from God he could join forces with Jesus. He was taught that he must be born again even to see the kingdom (John 3:1-5). James has already shown that some looked into the word or were hearers and did nothing.

Another question which is often raised by way of introduction to this passage is whether James is speaking about the initial act of justification in primary obedience to the gospel (becoming a Christian) or whether he is speaking of the fruits of good works in the Christian's life (as in James 3:17). The question is important because some would apply the principle of James to the discussion about baptism as a saving act of obedience (1 Peter 3:21; Acts 2:38; Mark 16:16) as proving that the faith of the alien must be expressed in a work of obedience to be "perfected" and justifying. Others argue that Paul had taught that justification is by faith without any work of obedience in being saved and that by "justify" in James 2 the author means "the declaring of righteousness" which belongs to the saved and that this is done by such works or good deeds as are the fruits of faith in the Christian's life, for example, feeding the hungry and clothing the naked.

This question is somewhat difficult to answer. Ropes thinks that James in 1:19-21 is speaking of a Christian's attention to the knowledge of God's word and not to initial acceptance of the gospel. But Ross applies it to such hearing of the gospel as that of the Bereans in Acts 17:11. The use of the word "justify" is thought by some to favor the idea of primary obedience, but in a passage like Galatians 5:4 it seems to refer to the activities of Christians. Too, Paul seems to speak of "salvation" to those members of the church (Phil. 2:15) as something dependent upon works—continued obedience to the will of Christ during the course of the Christian life. Strictly speaking, a Christian's justification or pardon from sin is conditioned in the New Testament upon repentance

What Does It Profit? JAMES 2:14

¹⁴What does it profit, my brethren, if a man says he has faith but has not works? Can his faith save him?

---

and confession of sins (1 John 1:7-9; Acts 8:22f.). But his continual acceptance by the Father is dependent upon his fruitful obedience to the truth. Hence it really makes little difference whether the passage is taken one way or the other. Paul's salvation without works included the obedience of faith (Rom. 1:5; Gal. 3:27). Though it seems that James and Paul are using the term "works" in different ways, still, if James is speaking of activity of the Christian life, he is talking about the principle of justification, which works in both areas.

[14] James begins his refutation of the erroneous idea that faith can save without works by pointing up the issue sharply with a series of questions in order to state his fundamental position that faith which does not result in works is vain, just as religion which is not lived out is vain (1:26).

What does it profit? means "What good is it to the man?" Compare Jesus' "What will it profit a man?" (Matt. 16:26). Paul asked the same question about his suffering. If there is no resurrection, "What is the profit?" The adjective is found in the Septuagint in Job 15:3. It is not that there is no profit in faith. James would never affirm this. Nor does James deny that one might really have faith without works. But he affirms that faith alone is without profit for a man, because it cannot result in his salvation.

One should not emphasize the **says he has faith** to imply that James means that one claims to have faith but really does not. It is essential to James' argument that one may be assumed to be a believer without being a worker. A faith which is not active may be unworthy of the name and of no value, but that does not mean that it is insincere. **Faith** is introduced without definition as the basic ingredient of the Christian life. A "believer" is a frequent name in the Bible for a Christian (Acts 16:1; 1 Tim. 5:16). James has already emphasized faith in his letter (1:3, 6; 2:1). He uses it in a general sense without regard to the subtleties or implications of meaning (e.g., "trust" or "endurance").

JAMES 2:14 *Works*

By **works** James means any obedience to the law of Christ as a Christian, but generally the term refers to "good deeds" or "conduct," the fruits of the Christian life (Matt. 5:16; 23:3; Rom. 2:6; John 3:20). In Titus 1:16 Paul uses it of conduct, consisting of many deeds over a period of time. James has already emphasized that the word of truth must continue to be looked into and "done." He has mentioned specifically such things as "visiting the orphans and widows" (1:21, 25, 26). Later he will say that the wise teacher must show "by his good life his works in meekness of wisdom" (3:13), and he specifies "full of mercy and good fruits" (3:17). Thus the reference is to such works which fulfil the law of liberty and by which men will be judged. James uses the same word as Paul in his statement that man is not justified by works (Rom. 3:28; 4:2), but he means something altogether different. Paul means meritorious works, such as those performed under the law, which have no relation to the blood of Christ and are performed as the basis or merit of justification in themselves. With James the idea is that a Christian who accepts Christ as his sacrifice and thus has God's righteousness imputed to him must live in obedience of faith to the law of Christ, manifesting his faith in works. Paul would have no quarrel with this. As a matter of fact, Paul is just as insistent on it. The Christian must work out his salvation (Phil. 2:12). He is created for good works (Eph. 2:9). He must present his members as instruments of righteousness (Rom. 6:13). Paul warned his readers who were Christians that "If you live according to the flesh, you will die" (Rom. 8:13). The Christian must bear fruit for God (Rom. 7:4). Paul himself is the one who coined the phrase "the obedience of faith" (Rom. 1:5; 16:26). Paul would never have denied that works of obedience to the law of Christ are necessary to make a Christian's faith perfect and saving.

Can his faith save him? James uses the word **faith** here with the article so as to mean "the kind just mentioned," that which has no works, or "faith alone." The question is asked in Greek in such a way as to expect a negative answer: James emphatically is asserting that such a faith (one which has not works) cannot save. **Save** here is to be taken in the same

Brother in Need — JAMES 2:15, 16

15If a brother or sister is ill-clad and in lack of daily food, 16and one of you says to them, "Go in peace, be warmed and filled," without giving them the things needed for the body, what does it profit?

---

sense as in 1:21. James means the future salvation which is still to be worked out by the man born again (cf. 1:18 with 21 and also 2 Thess. 5:23; 2 Peter 1:5).

[15] James begins his discussion of the merits of the claim for a non-working faith by an illustration in which he supposes a fellow Christian, a **brother or sister,** did not have the necessities of life. Hereby he emphasizes in a strong and concrete way the necessity of the *work* of faith. A Christian is under obligation to do good to all men, and especially to those who are of the household of faith (Gal. 6:10). Love is not to be in word only, but in deed as well (1 John 3:17, 18). James has just demonstrated that works of mercy are necessary toward the poor (2:13). **Ill-clad** is often used for scanty clothes (John 21:7) or clothes which are virtually none at all. The lack of clothing and food emphasizes the destitution of the fellow Christian. A Christian who does not rise to help his brother in such condition has not the love of God (1 John 3:17).

[16] James is thinking of any Christian who might speak these words of seeming concern for brethren. It is not to be thought that James means that those who argue that faith alone is sufficient for salvation are the ones who act this way. He is simply using an illustration to show such people that faith expressed in word only would be worthless. There are many who say and do not, just as there are many who look into the perfect law and do not obey it.

A similar farewell greeting occurs in Judges 18:6 (Ms. B); 2 Samuel 3:21; and Acts 16:36. The phrase means something like our English "keep well." The phrase indicates a real concern for the welfare of the needy. **Warmed** means warmed by good clothes (Job 31:20; Hag. 1:6). Thus James' words might be translated, "Keep well. Dress warmly and eat well."

The things needed are, of course, the food and clothing necessary to life. What value would your good blessing and

JAMES 2:17, 18 — *Faith by Itself*

17So faith by itself, if it has no works, is dead.

18But some one will say, "You have faith and I have works." Show me your faith apart from your works, and I by my works will show you my faith.

---

farewell be? They would not only be useless, but somewhat of a mockery. The application to the thought of the context is given in the next verse.

[17] James applies the illustration to the contention. Just as the answer to the needy man without deeds of charity would be profitless, so also faith **if it has no works** is useless. Faith's "having works" is to be thought of in the sense of having or including something in itself, and thus bringing it about or causing it. James has talked of patience having "full effect" (1:4); compare "fear has punishment" (1 John 4:18) and "confidence which has a great reward" (Heb. 10:35). Thus James means that faith may or may not lead to or be characterized by works or good deeds. Compare Paul's "work of faith" (1 Thess. 1:3). If it does not produce works or good deeds, it is of no value.

A faith which does not cause works is **dead.** James does not contrast faith and works, but a faith which is active and a dead faith which is not. The dead faith is idle or vain (vs. 20). This sense of **dead** to mean "idle" or "without value" is common: Revelation 3:1; Hebrews 6:1; 9:14; Romans 6:11; 7:8. James says that **by itself** it is dead, thus not able to accomplish anything. **By itself** probably means "as long as it remains or continues by itself" or alone. This is the usual meaning of the Greek phrase (cf. Acts 28:16). As long as faith is strictly **by itself,** it is valueless; the moment it acts it is no longer without works and is no longer dead or useless.

[18] The meaning of this verse seems plain, but it is difficult to explain in detail. Some commentators take the whole sentence as the saying of one contending that faith alone will save. Others take the first part to be the contention of such a one, but they take James' answer as beginning with "show me." In this view the man is simply a supposed objector, as in 1 Corinthians 15:35. Still others see the speaker as different from either James or the "faith only" man of

Faith Shown by Works JAMES 2:18

verse 14. Lenski makes the speaker someone who comes to James' readers and says that "you" (some Christian) have faith, and "I" (James) have works. It does not appear important to the thought to settle this point. It is clear that James is refuting the idea that one may be saved in one way, another by a different way.

The point of the statement **you have faith and I have works** is that one person may excel in one thing and another in still something else, but this does not mean that both may not be acceptable. Each man has his strong points. One man may be saved by his faith, another by his good deeds. Huther and others cannot see these words as coming from an objector who argues for "faith only," since, in this regard, the objector ought to say, "You have works and I have faith," instead of "You have faith and I have works." To avoid this he understands the speaker (like Lenski, above) to be someone different from both James and the man of verse 14. This man on the side might say to James' opponent, "You have faith and I (James) have works." Either way James is rejecting the contention that a one-sided insistence on faith or works will benefit.

Whichever way the former part of the sentence goes, **show me your faith apart from your works** seems to be the reply to the contention that one may have faith and another works. The challenge is to demonstrate or prove the existence of faith without works. How can it be done? If a man tells me that he will kill me if I don't surrender my wallet, how can I demonstrate that I believe him? I might believe he meant it and still value the contents so much that I would try to avoid parting with my wallet, but it would be hard to prove the presence of faith except by obeying the thief. There is a semantic sense in which some would argue that "real" faith must act and that, unless faith acts, it is not genuine. This is probably not James' point. Faith is *demonstrable* only through works.

I by my works will show you my faith is the logical and (to James) the only way to prove one's faith. The man who professes the faith of Christ and really works at the job of producing fruits to the name of Christ will never be doubted as being a sincere believer. He proves his faith by his works.

[19] You believe that God is one; you do well. Even the demons believe—and shudder.

One who boasts of his faith but never does anything about it would be doubted.

The use of the **you** in the refutation of an idea, in which the writer turns aside to address an imaginary opponent, is supposed to be evidence that James is patterning his document on the Greek diatribe style. But it is doubtful that James had ever seen or heard any such in reality. There are too many other possible parallels. The style is well known in rabbinical writings. The Old Testament style of the prophets in addressing their enemies could be James' model, if one is needed (see note on 5:1).

[19] Having taken care of his objector, James now goes to the heart of the argument over the relation of faith and works. Some commentators suppose that in this first concrete instance James touches on the idea that any Jew would claim for his justification—that he believed in the one God of Israel. Had not this belief in monotheism been the basis of Israel's salvation? This was the fundamental proposition in the Jews' confession of faith or Shema, which they prayed daily: Deuteronomy 6:4; Nehemiah 9:6; Isaiah 45:6; Matthew 23:9; Romans 3:30; 1 Corinthians 8:4, 6; and James 4:12. Compare Hermas, *Mandates* I.i.1, "Believe this first of all things, that God is one." This is the great and fundamental truth of all the Hebrew-Christian religion. But the belief of this alone is not enough.

James does not despise faith. It bears repeating that James, as Paul, takes faith to be the foundation and meritorious basis of our salvation. James would never belittle faith or any claim to faith. One who believes God is doing **well.** If he lets that faith do for him what it should, he is on his way to salvation. If not, then he is no better than the demons.

Demons were "evil spirits" under the service of Satan. They possessed people and in the gospel age were subject to the power of Jesus and the apostles acting in his name. The Gospels show that they recognized Jesus as the Holy one of

[20]Do you want to be shown, you shallow man, that faith apart from works is barren?

God and were tormented in his presence. They also **believe**. But there is no evidence that they can or will repent or express their faith so that they may be redeemed. If a man only believes, in what way is he better than the demons? The verb **shudder** originally meant to "bristle" (as Job 4:14f.). But it is used simply of one who stands in awe or reverence (Dan. 7:15). Here it may refer to the demons' fear of impending punishment.

The statements of the Bible about demons should not be attributed to superstition or mental diseases. God's word affirms their existence. It is no more difficult to believe in demons than to believe in God, Christ, the Holy Spirit, angels, or the devil. For passages that mention and assume the existence of such, see Luke 8:30; Matthew 11:18; Luke 7:33; John 7:20; 8:48f.; Matthew 12:24. The Bible hints (though it does not state plainly) that the demons were to be consigned to the abyss (Matt. 8:29; Luke 8:31). In 1 Timothy 4:1ff. false teaching is attributed to the influence of demons.

[20] The language calls upon the believer in "faith only" to be willing to recognize or acknowledge the truth. James is so confident of the truth of his position and of the force of his reasoning that he calls upon the errorists to concede. The man who will argue in such fashion as the above is **shallow** in James' mind. Thus James indicates his vexation at him. Beginning with this verse James presents the proof of his argument back to Abraham's justification.

Apart from works is a variation of "faith if it has no works." Compare Hebrews 4:15, "yet without sin" (without committing sin). Thus it is a faith which does not express itself in works. The manuscripts vary between **barren** and "dead," but "dead" is probably a scribal change to make it agree with verse 26. **Barren** comes originally from a word which means "unemployed" or "idle" (Matt. 20:3, 6; Titus 1:12). Then the word comes to mean "lazy" and "useless." It has no connection with the idea of fruit. "Useless" is probably the meaning here. Compare 2 Peter 1:8, "unfruitful

21Was not Abraham our father justified by works, when he offered his son Isaac upon the altar?

[useless] in the knowledge of Christ." It is useless to have faith if it does not express itself in obedience. Some commentators who think that James is refuting Paul refer the expression **you shallow man** to Paul. But James certainly did not have Paul's teaching in mind.

[21] James' first example is **Abraham.** The use of Abraham is due to his historical place in the Bible and also to the fact that he is the father of the Jews. His example of faithfulness was mentioned by Jewish writers. Sirach relates: "Abraham was a great father of many nations who . . . when he was proved was found faithful" (44:19f.). We also find in 1 Maccabees 2:52, "Was not Abraham found faithful in temptation, and it was imputed to him for righteousness?" Such quotations show that the matter of Abraham's faith was a familiar one to James' audience. New Testament writers also hold up the faith of Abraham as an example (see Heb. 11:8ff.; Gal. 3:6ff.; Rom. 4:3). As has been stated, it is possible that the point is raised because the Jews felt that being a descendant of Abraham or an orthodox believer was sufficient for salvation.

Justified is a key word here. It had two general meanings: (1) "To vindicate" or show that one's course is wise or just. This was a frequent meaning in the Old Testament, where God, by giving Israel victory in battle, justified her cause. Compare Matthew 11:19; Luke 7:35; 1 Timothy 3:16. (2) "To be acquitted or pronounced and treated as righteous" or innocent. This is termed the forensic or legal use of the word. This was also a frequent use in the Old Testament: Exodus 23:7; Deuteronomy 25:1; 1 Kings 8:32; Isaiah 5:23; 50:8; 53:11. New Testament passages which have this meaning, besides James and Paul, are Matthew 12:37 and Luke 18:14.

It has been contended that the first meaning is that of James here and that he means that Abraham was merely declared or proved righteous; that the course of God in blessing him and selecting him and giving him the promise earlier was vindicated or shown to be right by his action in offering his son. But this hardly does justice to James' argument. James is talking about faith *saving* a man (vs. 14). It is not contemplated merely that one already just or acquitted is proved or declared righteous, but the action of God in declaring him righteous is referred to.

The words **by works** declare the grounds or reasons for which Abraham was declared righteous. James used the plural word as he had previously done (vss. 14, 17, 18) because he is still thinking of the category of things by which one is saved (**works** along with "faith"), and the offering of **Isaac** is an instance. It is not Abraham's general conduct or whole life that is in point, but the one act of offering.

Other examples of Abraham's faith are mentioned: believing the promise of a son (Rom. 4:17-21); the departing from his native land (Heb. 11:8-12); the sacrificing of Isaac while thinking that he would be raised (Heb. 11:17-19). In Genesis 22:9ff. there is nothing said of "justification." But the offering was followed by a blessing's being pronounced upon him that his seed would be multiplied and all nations blessed through him "because you have obeyed my voice" (Gen. 22:16-18). From this James could easily infer the blessing of justification which had been connected with the earlier faith (Gen. 15:6). Later in Genesis it was said that the promises were reiterated "because Abraham obeyed my voice" (26:5). Thus James could see that (though it is not specifically stated) the Old Testament record indicated that acts of obedience had led Abraham to another declaration of righteousness before God. Thus the act (**works**) is shown to be the basis of his justification. This is not to say that his works alone saved him, which James would not have affirmed. James mentions only what has been left out or neglected by some. The two worked together, as James goes on to show.

In Greek James' question **Was not Abraham justified by works** is introduced by the negative particle which expects a "yes" answer. James is saying in a most emphatic way that Abraham was justified on the basis of **works**.

As has been shown, Abraham's offering of Isaac was the cause of a later or additional justification to that of Genesis 15:6. But Paul's use of the Genesis passage in Romans 4:2, 5

> **22You see that faith was active along with his works, and faith was completed by works,**

to affirm that Abraham was not justified by works and that "to one that does not work, but trusts him who justifies the ungodly, his faith is reckoned as righteousness" raises the question as to whether James and Paul contradict each other in their use of the words **justified by works** and "faith." This question must not be avoided. It has been claimed that Paul could never have stood for the contention that Abraham was justified on the ground of the work which accompanied and authenticated his faith.

It must be admitted that Paul and James use the word "justify" in the same sense (though talking about a different occasion of declaration of righteousness). But a contradiction is avoided by seeing that they used the word **works** in a different context or meaning. Paul is thinking of the works of the law of Moses as the basis of justification. Notice Galatians 2:16; 3:11; 5:4, where Paul adds "the law" to his denial that one is justified by works. He insists that Abraham's justification was before the law and apart from it, just as he insisted (Rom. 4:10ff.) that it was before circumcision. James is thinking of works of faith or obedience. That Paul would have denied this in the sense that James means it no one can say, for Paul did not deny it. Further, in Titus 3:5,7 Paul combines being justified by his (God's) grace with being saved by baptism as "the washing of regeneration." Thus it is not beyond Paul's thought that a work of obedience growing out of one's faith in God or Christ is the basis of justification.

[22] This statement may well be a question, though it is impossible to tell from the original. Either makes good sense in the context. As it stands in the text, it forms a conclusion to the deduction that Abraham was justified by works in offering Isaac. If it is a question, then James is asking the reader if this does not follow. James asks if the fact that faith "worked together with works" is not proved by the incident just mentioned. James demonstrates the mutual dependence of faith and works. Abraham's faith "cooperated with" or

23and the scripture was fulfilled which says, "Abraham believed God, and it was reckoned to him as righteousness"; and he was called the friend of God.

"aided" works (that is, to achieve their desired end—justification). The verb means to "cooperate with" or "help" someone. Paul used it thus in Romans 8:28 (cf. also 1 Cor. 16:16; 2 Cor. 6:1).

For the verb **completed** or "perfected" see Luke 13:32 and Acts 20:2f. James does not mean that Abraham had a faith which was imperfect or defective in itself so that real faith came about only after he had obeyed God's command. His faith was real before. But he means that Abraham's faith was not perfected or completed so that it did for him what God had intended it to do until after the obedience. The faith that he had was complemented or helped along by his work of obedience; they went hand in hand, with faith being made stronger by the tests to which it was put until in the great test of offering his son it reached perfection. Faith and works give each other elements of character that neither has alone. James does not teach works alone any more than he teaches faith alone. There is a work of faith (1 Thess. 1:5; Gal. 5:6) or an obedience of faith (Rom. 1:5; 16:25). When the two aid each other, faith accomplishes its end—justification.

[23] The **scripture** referred to is Genesis 15:6. What does James mean by **fulfilled**? Some say it means "confirmed" and that this statement was only confirmed in the offering of Isaac, not that justification actually took place then. But "confirmed" is not a meaning which can be ascribed to the verb. In such a context the verb refers to the fulfillment of God's predictions or promises in some future event. In the Old Testament this was its meaning (1 Kings 2:27). Its New Testament usage is abundant (Matt. 1:22; Luke 1:20; Acts 1:16). Even the promise of Jesus is said to have been fulfilled (John 18:9, 32).

It is true that the statement as it occurs in Genesis is not a prediction but a statement of fact. But James deduced (as we have shown) from the statements of Genesis 22:16-18 that a justification had taken place "because he had done this."

Huther says: "But as it notifies facts which point to later actions in which they received their full accomplishment, James might consider it as a word of promise which was fulfilled by the occurrence of these later actions." It is possible that a thing spoken at one time and fulfilled in a measure at one time may later receive another and more complete fulfillment. So James sees that the perfection of Abraham's faith in the offering of Isaac and the justification which is implied following it fulfil the statement of Genesis 15:6 of Abraham's faith and the reckoning for righteousness. It is no contradiction that Paul saw justification as taking place at the time of Genesis 15:6 also.

Genesis 15:6 originally referred to Abraham's belief that he would become the father of a seed. But it is also a general statement of Abraham's trustfulness exemplified by his whole life, as James sees in subsequent events.

The verb **reckoned** is frequently used in the Septuagint "to express what is equivalent to, having the like force and weight as something mentioned" (Knowling). Compare Isaiah 40:17 and Romans 2:26. The verb also has the meaning of crediting something to one's account which does not (properly) belong to him (Psalm 31 [32]: 2). Either of these senses will satisfy the meaning here. God took Abraham's faith instead of righteousness (which he did not have in the absolute, being a sinner); he thus credited to Abraham's account the righteousness which he did not before possess. This is equivalent to saying, as Paul had seen (Rom. 4:2ff.), that he was "justified" or declared righteous. This is practically the same as saying that he was forgiven of his sins because of his perfect faith. This remains with James, as well as Paul, the meritorious basis of man's salvation. James' point is that this faith reckoned for righteousness was fulfilled (at least in an additional measure) by the offering of Isaac.

Abraham *became* **the friend of God** as a result of his exercise of faith. He was not **called** the friend of God (at least not in scripture) until much later (cf. Isa. 41:8; 2 Chron. 20:7). His becoming the friend of God was a result of the expression of his faith in offering Isaac. He was justified by the deed and as a consequence also was referred to as God's friend.

Not by Faith Alone — JAMES 2:24, 25

²⁴You see that a man is justified by works and not by faith alone. ²⁵And in the same way was not also Rahab the harlot justified by works when she received the messengers and sent them out another way?

---

[24] This verse states the conclusion which James thinks all can see from what he has presented. He has fully demonstrated that it takes both **faith** and **works** to procure man's justification. Especially does he think that he has shown this from Abraham's case. It is clear that works growing out of his faith were the cause of the justification which followed his offering of his son. It was "because you have *done* this" that the blessing followed. So works justify, not in themselves alone, but still they justify.

To a man wishing to be saved by the "implanted word," the "word of truth" (James 1:18, 21), faith alone is not enough. Faith "by itself is dead," "is barren" (2:17, 20). As in Abraham's case faith must cooperate with works, and the works must complete and bring faith to its goal of justification. The stress is on the word **alone.** James could not deny that faith justified Abraham; the very passage in which he saw Abraham's work of offering as the "fulfillment" emphasized that "Abraham believed." James is thinking of a faith which exists "in" or "by" itself and apart from any expression or work. Since such a faith is "idle" and "useless," it cannot justify. Hence salvation or justification in the sense that works perfect faith is "by works" and not "by faith alone." Paul's use of "faith without works of the law" is quite different but perfectly in harmony with James.

[25] James now adds a case drawn from people other than the family of Abraham. The reason for this probably was to broaden the principle and to show that it operated outside the chosen Old Testament family. The principle includes every race, sex, and condition of life. Paul argues that anyone who comes to accept the principle of faith upon which Abraham was justified becomes in this sense a child of Abraham as he becomes "the father of all that believe" (Rom. 4:11; Gal. 3:7-9).

²⁶For as the body apart from the spirit is dead, so faith apart from works is dead.

Rahab was a Canaanite, a woman fallen under the weight of sin. Yet by believing in the God of Israel, of whom she had heard (Joshua 2:9ff.), and receiving the spies and sending them out another way, she walked in the steps of the faith which Abraham had (Rom. 4:12). In this way her acceptance with God is proved. She is listed among the Old Testament worthies (Heb. 11:31) and appears in the genealogy of Jesus Christ himself (Matt. 1:5). The details of her deeds are given in Joshua 2 and 6:23. The writer of Hebrews, as well as James, emphasized that her faith was demonstrated in "obedience" in receiving the spies. Her justification by works is therefore proved. Her faith cooperated with, or helped, her works and was perfected by what she did.

[26] James sees the whole case as made out and concludes the argument with another illustration. **For** is added as a particle of conclusion. This is grounds for saying what has been said already about **faith** and **works.** He is drawing the same conclusion as in verse 24. But he also repeats the statement of verse 17 that "faith by itself, if it has no works, is dead" and adds to it the illustration which gives it vividness.

The body is the human body, and **the spirit** is the animating principle of life, as in Ecclesiastes 12:7. When the spirit leaves the body, it dies and returns to the dust. From then on the body is nothing. So James insists that apart from works faith is dead. Faith not expressed in works is like the body which has been left by the spirit; it is a dead body. The sense of **dead** here is probably like that of "barren" or "idle" in verse 20; it is to be taken in the sense of "useless," unable to profit.

NOTES ON "FAITH ALONE"

The doctrine of "justification by faith only" has become a loaded expression in modern denominational theology. It is a real bone of contention. The modern denominational doctrine (in some groups) is that in conversion man is saved at the instant of faith, when he puts his trust in Christ as his

Faith Apart from Works　　　　　　　　　　JAMES 2:26

personal Savior. This leads to the denial of the efficacy of other acts of obedience, especially baptism. The Bible plainly teaches that baptism as an act of faith is a condition of salvation or remission of sins (justification). See Acts 2:38; Mark 16:16; 1 Peter 3:21; Acts 22:16. This does not mean that baptism is sacramental in the sense in which sacraments are generally understood. A sacrament (as used in Catholicism) is an act which has efficacy in itself and in the validity of the administrator (an authorized person) and requires no faith on the part of the one on whom it is administered. In such an act faith does not "work together," for there is no faith.

But this use of the term "faith only" is not the historic meaning of the term. Martin Luther did not mean this by his formula, and to attribute the rise of the term in its denominational sense to him (as is so often done) is an injustice. Luther meant that faith is the only meritorious ground of justification—salvation or remission of sins can never be obtained on any grounds apart from faith in Jesus' blood. There are only two means of salvation as Paul stated them in Romans 3:27: "the principle" (law) of faith and the "principle" (law) of human works of merit (such as those under the law). See NEB on this verse. Since Paul rejected the principle of works, it follows that, unless one is to be saved by the principle of faith, he cannot be saved. This expression did not originate with Luther; others had used it before him. But he stoutly defended the translation of Romans 3:28: "Man is justified without the works of the law through faith only." To deny this (to Luther) would be to deny the whole teaching of Paul and to affirm that one can be saved by his own works without the Lord Jesus. In this understanding Luther is correct.

But Luther himself emphasized the importance of baptism. He is quoted as saying, "We are justified by faith alone, but not by the faith which is alone." Some of the harshest things which Luther ever said were said in one edition of his commentary—against those who deny the place of baptism in the New Testament.

Thus we see that "faith only" can be used in two senses. It can be used *compositely* as the principle of justification. But it can be used *analytically*, where the process of obedience is broken down into its component parts. In the first sense, salvation is by "faith only"; in the second sense, it is "by works and not by faith only," for here faith is only one of the conditions of pardon: "He who *believes* and is *baptized* will be saved" (Mark 16:16); "*Repent* and be *baptized* . . . for the forgiveness of your sins" (Acts 2:38). Thus the doctrine of salvation at the moment of faith—without obedience—is not a biblical teaching, and it does not take its roots from the reformers. It is rooted in the conversion experience theology of early revivalism. It sets aside the plain teaching of the Bible on the doctrine of obedience and works of faith.

It is easy to see, therefore, that there is no contradiction between Paul's use of justification by faith (only or "without works") and James' teaching that justification is by works and not by faith only. Paul is thinking of the composite nature of faith as the principle of justification by faith rather than by the works of the law (or of human merit). James is thinking analytically of faith as a condition of justification and insists that it must obey the conditions of the teaching of Christ and perfect itself in works.

ADMONITION TO TEACHERS, 3:1-18

Chapter 3 treats of two subjects directly related to each other: The bridling of the tongue (a metonymy for "speech," compare "what he says" in vs. 2) and the analysis of true wisdom. These subjects both refer to the teacher; the first part relates to his responsibility and control of his speech (3:1-12) and the second to the teacher's wisdom (3:13-18). That verses 1-12 are to be interpreted in this manner is quite plain. But the second point must be deduced from the context. It appears that "the one wise and understanding" of verse 13 also describes the teacher. For the evidence see the commentary on verse 13. Ropes says, "Chapter 3 relates to the teacher and wise man. That the two are treated as substantially identical is significant." Wisdom and speech are connected in Proverbs 31:26, "She opens her mouth with wisdom, and the teaching of kindness is on her tongue."

Controlling the Tongue   JAMES 3:1

[1] Let not many of you become teachers, my brethren, for you know that we who teach shall be judged with greater strictness.

James is demanding that the Christian allow the gospel of Christ to impose this rule upon him.

Bridling the Tongue, 3:1-12

In James 3:1-12 James returns to a subject mentioned in chapter 1:19, 26. There he had said, "Be quick to hear, slow to speak." In a sense, chapter 1:19-27 is a development of proper hearing; in the present section the proper attitude toward speech is developed. In 1:26 lack of control of the tongue is mentioned as proof of the absence of practical application of religion that made religion vain. The whole subject is now enlarged. There may also be implied (in the view of the plea for consistency in vs. 9) that this proper use of the tongue is to be connected in development with the consistency in faith (partiality) and demonstration of faith (faith and works). Self-control and meekness of wisdom are further indications of pure religion or a part of one's works as a Christian by which justification is achieved. As Paul would have said it, this is a part of working out our salvation as obedient children (Phil. 2:12, 15).

[1] Teachers here must certainly be seen against the background of Jewish rabbinical tradition. **Teacher** here equals "rabbi." The rabbis were local teachers in the synagogues. They were also called "lawyers" and "scribes." The contemporary records show that the position was esteemed as one of honor and prestige and desired as an end in itself. Jesus criticized those who loved "being called rabbi" (Matt. 23:7, 8). The criticism is probably due to the fact that the position was used to exercise power over others. Jesus saw the charge that he was in league with Beelzebub as an attempt to turn the multitude against him and thus considered it a misuse of the tongue. He said, "By your words you will be justified, and by your words you will be condemned" (Matt. 12:37). Compare also Romans 2:19f.

JAMES 3:1

Some form of the title rabbi was often applied to Jesus: Mark 9:5; 11:21; 14:45; John 1:38; 3:2; 4:31; 6:25. In the church the office of teacher seems (as in our modern Bible classes) to have depended upon ability to teach (Titus 2:3, 4) and not on official appointment. Teachers are mentioned in 1 Corinthians 12:28; Acts 13:1; and Ephesians 4:11. In 1 Corinthians 14:26-40 we have a passage which is especially instructive. Teaching (vs. 26), along with the exercise of spiritual gifts, seems to have been the privilege of those wishing to rise to speak. The author of Hebrews insists that all disciples by reason of time "ought to be teachers" (Heb. 5:12). The exercise of the right in the assembly was denied women (1 Cor. 14:34; 1 Tim. 2:12), but opportunity for them to instruct must have been found in other circumstances (1 Cor. 11:5; Titus 2:3f.). Teachers were distinguished from prophets only in that the latter were inspired teachers.

With all the encouragement to teach in the New Testament, it is evident that the prohibition here against letting **many become teachers** is not due to an excess of teachers or to any discouraging of the proper ambition to teach. James is warning of the dangers inherent in the responsibility of teaching, especially in view of the confusion and vileness (vss. 13ff.) resulting at times from the misuse of the position. All teachers, among whom James classes himself, will bear heavy responsibility for their influence, due to their power in the eternal destiny of men whom they affect for good or ill. James, therefore, is saying in effect, "Don't many of you become teachers, if you are not certain that you can control your tongue, that your teaching ministry will yield peaceable results and that you are willing to shoulder the responsibility for your work."

The word **judged**, which may be either good or bad, has the adverse meaning in passages like Mark 12:40. The word may here signify censure for failure in duty, as it seemingly does in Romans 13:2 or 1 Corinthians 11:29. In these passages, of course, the censure may be accompanied by penalty. Thus this passage may mean that the offending teacher may be condemned at the last judgment for not having lived up to his stewardship as a teacher. The one who

A Perfect Man — JAMES 3:2

²For we all make many mistakes, and if any one makes no mistakes in what he says he is a perfect man, able to bridle the whole body also.

knows and does not will receive heavier judgment (Luke 12:47ff.). One in the position of teacher is certainly assumed to know the Master's will. Hence, the teacher must be prepared for greater censure and penalty for failing. The teacher proclaims God's will and must proclaim it as God desires (1 Peter 4:11; Gal. 1:10f.). He will be judged on how well he does this.

[2] James says that we all are guilty of many kinds of faults and offenses. He says, **We all make many mistakes** —literally, "we all stumble with respect to many things" (see 2:10; 2 Peter 1:10; Jude 24). That sin is universal is an almost axiomatic assertion of the scriptures. It is also of universal admission. "All have sinned and fall short of the glory of God" (Rom. 3:23). "If we say we have no sin, we deceive ourselves, and the truth is not in us" (1 John 1:8). There is no human infallibility. James' point is that, since this is true, it is clear that we should avoid (on any but the noblest motives) the taking up of the calling which brings the greatest responsibility and the greatest temptation of all to sin.

The sins of the tongue seem to be the most prevalent of all sins and the most difficult to avoid. There is probably a bit of hyperbole (exaggeration for emphasis) in the following verses of James, just as there is in Paul's representation of the love of money as "root of all evils" (1 Tim. 6:10). If a person could be found who does not make a mistake in word (in his speech), he would indeed be a remarkable man. Either in teaching or in wicked or empty speech all have sinned. For the thought compare Sirach 19:16, "Who is the one not sinning with his tongue?"

The comment on James 1:4 explains that the word **perfect** means "attaining its end or purpose, complete, nothing lacking." Ethically it means a "mature," a "full-grown," "well-rounded" person. Specifically it means that the kind of character which God is trying to develop in all of us as we grow into the image of Christ has been achieved. This does

JAMES 3:2-4 — *Bridle*

³If we put bits into the mouths of horses that they may obey us, we guide their whole bodies. ⁴Look at the ships also; though they are so great and are driven by strong winds, they are guided by a very small rudder wherever the will of the pilot directs.

---

not necessarily mean a sinless man, though in this passage in view of James' idea of its difficulty, it approaches that. The idea is that the man who has mastered the most difficult task can certainly do the less difficult. Hence the one not sinning in word must be all that God desires in a Christian.

Able to bridle the whole body also is amplification of the principle just explained. It is almost apposition. Since one has controlled what James will describe as the most unruly member, he certainly must be able to subject all the other members of the body, as eyes, hands, stomach. The use of the term **bridle** prefigures the illustration of bridling the horses in the next verse. In Matthew 5:29 we have another use of one member at odds with the whole body.

[3] This verse is a simple illustration. As one controls the body of a horse by controlling his mouth, so, if we can control our speech, we can regulate the entire body. The application of the illustration is left unexpressed but it is plain from the context.

[4] The word rendered **look at** serves to enliven a narrative and to call attention or consideration to something. James uses it six times: 3:4, 5; 5:4, 7, 9, 11. The **also** calls attention to a second illustration: "In addition to horses, consider ships, too." **Ships** were a common sight on the seas of the Mediterranean world. They were **so great** in fact to carry many people (Acts 27:37), but even larger in relation to the small rudder.

For the **strong winds** on the seas, consider Jesus' experience (Matt. 14:24) and Paul's on the Mediterranean (Acts 27-28). A blowing wind in a storm is indeed rough or harsh, yet a ship uncontrolled in the face of such powers may be controlled by a **very small** instrument.

The verb **guided**, in James' characteristic style, repeats the verb of verse 3. Even in winds which may blow unfavorably a

⁵So the tongue is a little member and boasts of great things. How great a forest is set ablaze by a small fire!

ship may make progress by the use of the sails and **rudder** (by what is called "tacking"). The **rudder** was a steering paddle or oar. It worked in the back of the ship or through a porthole. In Acts 27:47 the word is plural because the ship often had two paddles fastened by a crossbar and was worked by two men.

The **will** means "desire," "inclination," or "impulse." It is the word whence comes our English word "hormone." Wherever the steersman intends for the ship to go, the rudder can direct the boat. The word **pilot** is a substantive participle, "the one guiding straight," and not the technical word for a "pilot" or "governor" of a ship. The one who holds the rudder can turn the ship about and thus control it.

[5] The **tongue** here is the literal member of the body, a small unit indeed of our bodies. But the **tongue** is used here by metonomy for the thing it does; it is the organ of speech. The **tongue** is little, like the rudder of the ship; but, just as the rudder can determine the course of the large ship, so the **tongue** has power to influence man's whole course and destiny. There is more on this in the following verses.

The damage such a little member can do is so great that it **boasts** of its power and influence. The tongue might say to all the larger members of the body, "I can determine the course of all of you. Let all take note of my power." James shows that unfortunately such a boast is not an idle one. For the use of such a personification by which one member of the body (like the tongue here) is individualized and shown to influence the whole body compare Matthew 5:29f.; 15:19; 1 John 2:16.

The Greek literally has the following play on words: "What size fire kindles what size forest!" It is left to our knowledge that the fire is very small on the one hand, but the thing burned is very large. One has only to envision a small match, a spark, or a cigarette lighting a fire which may burn over a whole forest of possibly millions of acres to grasp the vividness of the illustration. Many Old Testament passages as

> **⁶And the tongue is a fire. The tongue is an unrighteous world among our members, staining the whole body, setting on fire the cycle of nature,**[b] **and set on fire by hell.**[c]
>
> [b] Or *wheel of birth*
> [c] Greek *Gehenna*

---

well as classical passages utilize the same figure: Isaiah 9:18; 10:16-18; Zechariah 12:6; Psalm 83:14. Little things often have great power. So a careless word can consume a whole church. Compare Paul's figure of a church devouring itself (Gal. 5:15).

[6] The editors of the Greek texts and translators differ slightly over the way the words here are to be arranged. Whatever the arrangement, the language describes the tongue as a **fire** and **an unrighteous world.**

Like the small **fire** which kindles a whole forest, so the tongue is a fire (a use of a metaphor rather than a simile "like a fire"). The tongue may as completely destroy the whole body as the fire a forest.

An unrighteous world is literally "a world of unrighteousness." Just as we say, "There is a world of wisdom in that statement," so that phrase means there is a very large sum here (perhaps even the sum total), that is, the whole universe or compass of the thing. Thus James says that the tongue is the whole world of iniquity. The phrase is an assertion (somewhat hyperbolic) that the tongue is a universe of evil in itself. It voices every evil feeling and every kind of sinful thought; it sets in motion or gives concreteness to every kind of sinful act. Nothing evil is beyond its power of accomplishment. As has already been pointed out, this is comparable to Paul's thought of the love of money (1 Tim. 6:10). Both illustrations are to be understood in their contexts as slight hyperbole. James and Paul do not contradict each other. The fault which each is combatting is so powerful as a source of evil that figuratively it may be said to constitute the whole story.

Is is somewhat weak here for the place of the tongue **among our members.** The verb means "be appointed," "be constituted," "made," or "caused to be." Compare James 4:4, "Whoever wishes to be a friend of the world *makes* (constitutes) himself an enemy of God," and 2 Peter 1:8. Thus the tongue is made to be or is constituted a world of iniquity among our members, being so made that it is able to produce all the sins of the catalog.

This one member is able to bring the whole body to contamination or stain. **Staining** is used elsewhere only in Jude 23 (Greek). **Fire** is not usually thought defiling or staining; thus there is some mixing of metaphors. James' point is that as the fire can destroy the whole, so the tongue can defile the whole by inflaming the whole body and bringing it to sin.

The Greek has all this in modifying participial phrases all descriptive: "the fire, the world of unrighteousness—the one staining the whole body, both setting on fire . . . and being set on fire." It is hard to reproduce the vividness and expressiveness of the original. It has often been remarked that James was a close observer of natural phenomena.

The words **cycle of nature** are difficult; they seem to mean "the whole course of life": "The whole round or course of life is set on fire or inflamed by the tongue." This is a way of saying that the evil spreads from the tongue like a fire to all the members, appetites, and passions of man's whole nature or life. Lenski interprets: We are a part of the wheel of existence; we do not live isolated lives but affect others by what we do or say. Hence the tongue of one person sets in motion a flame (for example, gossip, lying, profanity) which then spreads destruction to others like a house in a city which catches fire and by spreading burns the whole town. (So also Mayor, who thinks that the meaning is "to stir up one person against another, one class against another, one nation against another, etc., until the entire complex of existence is affected.) Some such idea is what is meant.

The complexity of interpretation is due to the fact that the terms used by James may have more than one meaning. **Nature** may mean "birth" or "origin" (Luke 1:14) or "existence," as in James 1:23. The other term may be accented in two ways in Greek and may mean either "wheel" or "a course" or "path." It was used in the Orphic Mysteries with the sense of "the wheel of human origin," where men were thought of as being caught up in a continuing repetition of reincarnations as a succession of renewals of the world would occur. But such ideas could hardly be attributed to James. He must refer to the whole course of one's existence, the whole course of life about him, or the whole circle of his own members. In some way he is saying that everything around man seems affected by the tongue.

Such a **fire** as that just described could have its origin only in the fires of **hell.** This is a figurative use of the word **hell.** Only fire such as that pictured in the lake of fire, the second death, could light such a destructive fire as that spread by the tongue. Compare James' use in 3:15 of the wisdom producing strife, etc., as being "devilish" or Paul's description in 1 Timothy 4:1 of the teaching of false teachers as being inspired by demons. Jesus traced evil speech to the heart (Matt. 15:19). James shows that the evil heart is influenced by **hell.**

This is the only use of the Greek *Gehenna* outside of the Gospels (Matt. 5:22, 29, 30; 10:28; 18:9; 23:15, 33; Mark 9:43, 45, 47; Luke 12:5). The KJV translated three words by the same English word "hell": *Hades* ("the unseen world, the intermediate state where the spirit awaits the resurrection), *Gehenna* (literally, "the Valley of Hinnom," but signifying a place of torment after death for man's spirit), and *Tartarus* (the lower part of Hades, where the wicked dead are punished—cf. Job 41:20; *Enoch* 20:2; Josephus, *Against Apion* II, 240; and only 2 Peter 2:4 in the New Testament). The Greek thought regarding these places differed from that revealed in the New Testament only in that they knew of Hades and Tartarus alone (with the latter as the place of punishment for the wicked) and in that they thought of the states of the dead in these places as permanent (with no hope of a resurrection). Like the concept of Paradise (2 Cor. 12:4; Luke 23:43), the Greeks thought of the good as enjoying happiness in Hades. The New Testament enlarges upon the use of these terms by showing that the states are only between death and the resurrection. The new term *Gehenna* is used of the final and eternal place of torment.

Gehenna is the Greek form of the Hebrew *ge-hinnom* which means the "Valley of Hinnom" (Joshua 15:8; 18:16). It is also called Topheth (2 Kings 23:10).

Gehenna

The Valley of Hinnom was the place of the idolatrous worship of Molech, the fire god (2 Chron. 28:3; Jer. 7:31; 32:35; 2 Chron. 33:6; Lev. 18:21). As a result it was "defiled" by King Josiah (2 Kings 23:10) and became a place of refuse and abomination.

The association with the valley was not the source of the idea of a place of eternal spiritual punishment by fire. That concept occurs throughout the Old Testament (cf. Deut. 32:22; Lev. 10:2; Isa. 30:27, 30, 33; 33:14; 66:24; Dan. 7:10; Ps. 18:8; 50:3; 97:3). Jeremiah prophesied evil against the Valley of Hinnom (Jer. 19:2-10), and the concept of punishment by fire combined with this to develop a belief in a place of spiritual punishment to which the dread name Gehenna (already conditioned as a place of abomination) was given. The application of the place name follows the analogy of using such Palestinian places as Armageddon (Rev. 16:16; Zech. 13:11), Jerusalem (Gal. 4:26; Rev. 21:2), or Sodom (Rev. 11:8) for spiritual concepts.

Jewish literature shows that the idea was prevalent (*Enoch* 10:12-14, "sinners . . . will be led to the abyss of fire in torture and in prison they will be locked up for all eternity"; compare also 18:11-16; 27:1-3; Judith 16:17; 2 Esdras 7:36; Sirach 7:17; *Sibylline Oracles* 1:10:3; Mishna, Aboth 1:6; 1 Qumran M 2:8; *Assumption of Moses* 10:10). Some Jewish writers thought the chosen people would be exempt and that the duration would be limited. Philo taught, however, that evil Jews would be included and that the punishment was eternal (*On Rewards and Punishments* XXVI.152). The spiritual nature of Gehenna is shown by the fact that the Jews placed it in the Third Heaven (*Ascension of Isaiah* 4:14; *2 Enoch* 40:12; 41:2).

It is in the teaching of Jesus that the doctrine is most explicitly identified and affirmed. He spoke of **Gehenna** as a place of future punishment (Matt. 5:29; 18:8, 9; Mark 9:45, 47; 12:5); of the "Gehenna of fire" (Matt. 5:22); of destroying "both body and soul in Gehenna" (Matt. 10:28); of "being sentenced to Gehenna" (Matt. 23:33); of making one "a child of Gehenna" (Matt. 23:15). But the concept of this eternal spiritual punishment of the wicked is found frequently:

JAMES 3:7, 8 — *Tamed*

⁷For every kind of beast and bird, of reptile and sea creature, can be tamed and has been tamed by humankind, ⁸but no human being can tame the tongue—a restless evil, full of deadly poison.

2 Thessalonians 1:7-9; Romans 2:7-9; 2 Peter 3:7; Hebrews 12:29; Revelation 14:10; 19:20; 20:10, 14. The New Testament clearly teaches that the punishment suffered in Gehenna will be eternal (Mark 9:47, 48; Matt. 25:46; Rev. 14:11).

[7] All creatures are subject to being controlled and **tamed**, but by human efforts the tongue seems to be uncontrollable. The **for** points to the fact that this statement contains the evidence for the preceding statement of the hellish source of the tongue's evil. That it (of all creatures) cannot be **tamed** by man is proof of the tongue's perverseness. It is more vicious than any of the wild creatures. The verb **tamed** is used elsewhere in the New Testament only in Mark 5:4, of subduing demons.

James says **every kind of**, meaning "every individual nature" (qualitative) of beast, etc. So the expression means simply "all animals, birds, and fishes." The enumeration of living creatures in this way (classifying all living creatures except man) is based upon the Greek Old Testament (Gen. 1:26; 9:2; 1 Kings 4:33).

[8] **No human being** is able to subdue the **tongue** as it can wild creatures. Augustine interpreted this to mean that if it is ever done it must be done by divine help. Such help from God may be had by prayer. Only in this way may we hope to "keep our tongue from evil" (Ps. 34:13; cf. 141:3; 1 Peter 3:10). Augustine's view seems to bring out the force of the "no one of man" accurately.

Restless here is the same word James used in 1:8 of the unstable man. The sense "unstable" or "inconsistent" could apply here as agreeing with the inconsistent action of both blessing and cursing in verse 9. But the vividness of the figure of the tongue as a wild and restless evil, which like a caged beast never is still but walks back and forth, back and forth, is striking and is probably the meaning. How like this is the

JAMES 3:8, 9

⁹With it we bless the Lord and Father, and with it we curse men, who are made in the likeness of God.

wagging tongue of gossip, of profanity, or the mouthing of a conceited hobbyist, speculator, or false teacher. But the restlessness is not mere restlessness; it is **restless evil.** Not merely disagreeable, the tongue is **evil,** bringing sin.

For **full of deadly** (deathbearing) **poison** compare "full of adultery" (2 Peter 2:14); "full of envy" (Rom. 1:29). Undoubtedly the term is drawn from Psalm 140:3 (58:4) quoted in Romans 3:13, "The venom of asps is under their lips."

This is the last of James' vivid metaphors describing the great influence of small things like the tongue.

[9] In verses 9-12 James points to the inconsistency of the tongue (as he has just demonstrated its wickedness). We **bless the Lord and Father** with it and thus profess ourselves his children. Yet we **curse men** who are made in his likeness and are his children in another sense. Even nature is more consistent than this. James chooses this inconsistent cursing of our fellowmen as one of the improper uses of the tongue. He might have chosen many others.

The verb **bless** means customarily to "praise or extol someone," as in a eulogy, prayer, or song of praise (see Luke 1:64). It also means "to give thanks" (Mark 14:22; Matt. 26:26; 1 Cor. 14:16). The opposition with "curse" shows that the meaning of "praising" or "extolling" is the proper one.

To **curse** is to put someone under an imprecation, to invoke evil or, even sometimes, damnation upon him. This is what we do when we "damn" someone. The incongruous combination of blessing and cursing is often noted (Ps. 62:4; Rom. 12:13; 1 Cor. 4:12).

Who are made in the likeness of God makes the inconsistency stand out. The Greek echoes the exact wording of the Greek Old Testament in Genesis 1:26.

The argument is that, since man bears the image or likeness of God, to harm him is in a sense the same as harming God. So for this reason one must not kill (Gen. 9:6), oppress the poor (Prov. 14:31; cf. Matt. 25:35) or hate his brother (1 John 4:20).

JAMES 3:10-12 — *Blessing and Cursing*

¹⁰From the same mouth come blessing and cursing. My brethren, this ought not to be so. ¹¹Does a spring pour forth from the same opening fresh water and brackish? ¹²Can a fig tree, my brethren, yield olives, or a grapevine figs? No more can salt water yield fresh.

---

[10] The mixture of **cursing** proves the unreality or insincerity of **blessing** (cf. Matt. 12:34, 23f.). No curse of our own can be pronounced by a Christian upon a fellowman without reflecting the curse upon the God whose image man bears. Only the curses which God himself has pronounced upon the men whom he has had to curse may a Christian repeat (such as 1 Cor. 16:22; Gal. 1:9). Otherwise he usurps God's place as judge and reviles God. "How can I curse whom God has not cursed?" (Num. 23:8).

The **so** is somewhat redundant, but it sums up what James has said about the combining of blessing and cursing with an uncontrolled tongue. Inconsistency ought not to exist in such a fashion.

[11] As is characteristic James enforces his argument with illustrations drawn from nature. Nature is not so incongruous that one may expect contradictory produce from the same sources. He begins his Greek sentence with an introductory interrogative particle which expects a negative answer: "A fountain does not send forth . . . does it?" Compare the use of the same particle in 2:14, "Can that faith save?" Thus James pointedly rejects his own hypothetical illustration. Such could not be; yet Christians were doing what was comparable to it.

The words **fresh water and brackish** are usual for a **spring** (fountain) of water (Rev. 8:10; 14:7; 16:4) or a cleft or opening (cf. Heb. 11:38). **Brackish** means "bitter water," "salty" (cf. Ex. 15:23; Rev. 8:11).

[12] Again, James begins verse 12 with the particle expecting a negative answer: "A fig tree cannot, can it . . . ?" **Figs, olives,** and **grapevine** were all very common in Palestine. It was a common saying that a tree must bear fruit after its kind (Gen. 1:11; and cf. Matt. 7:16, 20; 12:33). One would not expect to find a mixture of fruit on one tree. Yet

The Wise Teacher

¹³Who is wise and understanding among you? By his good life let him show his works in the meekness of wisdom.

the fruit of the lips of James' readers was a mixture of blessings and cursings.

The Greek word for **salt** (water) may mean "a spring," but elsewhere in the Bible it is used only as an adjective describing the Dead Sea as the "Salt Sea" (Num. 34:12; Deut. 3:17).

The Truly Wise Teacher, 3:13-18

This portion of the third chapter of James is best interpreted as a continuation of the subject begun in verse 1 on the influence and use of the tongue. After mentioning teachers in the first verse, James digresses in a sense to the more specific subject of the tongue's influence and evil. In verse 13 he reverts to the subject of verse 1 (the teacher). Under the contrast of heavenly and earthly wisdom he sets forth the deadliness of the sins of the tongue of the unwise teacher and the beauty of righteousness as the fruit of the truly wise teacher. There is abundant evidence that the term "wise man" is to be taken in the sense of "teacher." The truly wise teacher will have his fruit in peace and understanding leading to righteousness, and not in faction, jealousy, and vile deeds. This is an admonition which every individual who teaches or preaches God's word needs to study and take to heart. He should ask whether the fruit of his ministry indicates that his wisdom is from above or below. He may be sure that if faction, strife, and division follow his work, the source is not the "wisdom from above."

[13] The words **wise and understanding** are connected in Deuteronomy 1:13, referring to judges. The term "wise man" was frequently used of learned men such as philosophers and teachers (Rom. 1:14, 22; 1 Cor. 1:19, 26ff.; 3:20). It was used in the New Testament for the Jewish teachers (Matt. 11:25; Luke 10:21) and by Jesus to describe the teachers whom he would send out (Matt. 23:34). Jesus' use in the last passage is in the same sense as that of James in this passage.

This usage does not mean that James infers that wisdom is the possession of the teacher alone, but as a rule the teacher gained the reputation of having more skill and knowledge than the ordinary man. The argument is that, since this is true, he should show by his conduct that it is true in fact. The word **understanding** means "skilled" or "scientific" as opposed to what is untrained or unskilled (cf. Heb. 5:14). James' point is that the reputation of Christian teachers as wise and skilled men is to be justified in a practical way by their deeds and influence.

The sense of the verb **let him show** (as in 2:18 and Acts 10:28) is "prove" or "demonstrate." A tree is known by its fruits, a principle which James has alluded to in the preceding verses.

Life means "conduct," or "manner of life" (literally one's turnings or "meanderings" in life). In Latin the word *conversatio* meant the same and from this came the term "conversation." It earlier in English meant "conduct," but it is now limited to speech, so the rendering is no longer adequate (see also 1 Peter 2:15 and Gal. 1:13). The term translated **good** means "excellent," "noble," "beautiful or ideal" conduct. This is the kind expected of all Christians. The sense of the passage would be that of conduct which manifests real goodness.

"Let him prove by his conduct that he has meekness, doing what he does in the kind of meekness or humility that comes from wisdom." If the teacher's deeds are the right kind (and James goes on to develop this), they will be characterized by **meekness** and such meekness as will demonstrate that **wisdom** is present. A lack of meekness proves a lack of wisdom.

As an ethical attitude **meekness** means "gentleness," "humility," "courtesy," and "consideration toward others"; it is the opposite of a rough, egotistic, unyielding attitude. Notice how James elaborates on the right attitude in verse 17. Passages elsewhere in the New Testament which illustrate the usage include 1 Corinthians 4:21; 2 Corinthians 10:1; Titus 3:2; Galatians 6:1; and 2 Timothy 2:25.

Jealousy — JAMES 3:13, 14

¹⁴But if you have bitter jealousy and selfish ambition in your hearts, do not boast and be false to the truth.

On the word **wisdom**, see comment on 1:5. Here against the background of the Old Testament it is used for practical good judgment or common sense in the face of the concerns and duties of life, especially as those judgments are shaped by the teachings of God's word. **Meekness** is coupled with teaching in the Old Testament: Psalm 25:9. It is not only the wise who know how to receive instruction (Prov. 12:15), but the wise teacher also knows both what kind of counsel to give and how to give it (Prov. 11:14; 17:28; 29:9).

[14] The man whose conduct reveals **jealousy and selfish ambition** shows that wisdom is missing. Notice that James assumes that **jealousy and selfish ambition** are opposite in character to the deeds of wisdom. The wise man will never produce such fruits.

Jealousy in Greek is a neutral word and may have either a good sense of zeal or ardor (2 Cor. 7:7; 11:2) or the bad sense of envy or jealousy (as in 1 Cor. 3:3; 2 Cor. 12:20; Gal. 5:20). The use of the descriptive adjective **bitter** and the connection with **selfish ambition** (vss. 14, 16) show that James has the bad sense in mind here. The word **bitter** means "harsh" and refers to the feeling of anger or animosity inherent in such jealousy. James likely refers to the **jealousy** between the teachers in the local churches (his so-called "wise men") in their vying for positions and seeking for honors and the praise of their hearers. Or one might think of the following chapter and the questions concerning the causes of wars and fightings among the readers. **Jealousy** can certainly provoke bitter feeling and strife. The attitudes of jealousy and strife were much in evidence among the Jews on a national level, especially in the party bickerings and cleavage in the years preceding the outbreak of the Jewish wars. The rise of the Zealot party and the revolution which brought on the destruction of Jerusalem in A.D. 70 by the Roman army sharply divided the Jewish people and produced bickering and strife.

15This wisdom is not such as comes down from above, but is earthly, unspiritual, devilish.

Selfish ambition is a word of uncertain meaning. Moffatt and Goodspeed have "rivalry." It has been customary to derive the word from *eris* meaning "strife" or "discord." In Galatians 5:20 and 2 Corinthians 12:20 this word is found with *eris* and thus it has been argued that they are not related. But some writers still hold to this meaning and would translate "strife" or "contention," especially in view of the use in Philippians 1:17 and 15. On the other hand, the classical meaning is that of unethical political seeking. This seems to fit the context of all the New Testament uses: Philippians 1:17; 2:3; Romans 2:8; 2 Corinthians 12:20; Galatians 5:20.

Hearts (cf. 1:26, "deceives his heart") is used in the Bible as the seat of the faculty of thinking and so of moral and religious actions. See also James 4:8 and Matthew 15:19. If a man has these attitudes in his heart, they will come out in "disorder and every vile practice" (vs. 16). Actions proceed from the heart. The pretense of wisdom when the heart and life are not right is valueless and under such circumstances is a lie.

A pretense of wisdom is a **boast,** especially if it shows itself in a gloating over another on grounds of superiority. Such in effect is the wearing of the name "wise man" as a designation of a teacher. But if one does not demonstrate the wisdom in actual life, he should not bear the title or pretend to be wise; such a boast is really then a lie against the truth. **Truth** here means either simply "what is true"—his actual condition (the article being used with the abstract noun) or "the Gospel truth." The former explanation seems preferable. For one to pose as a wise man is a lie against reality when the fruit of foolishness is so plainly manifested.

[15] A **wisdom** which produced jealousy and selfish ambition (or strife), if it could be called wisdom at all, would be wisdom of the wrong kind. James is here ironic—this would not in the terms of biblical teaching be wisdom. A man with great learning and knowledge and with potential skill in imparting his ideas might be exceedingly wicked in his heart.

Earthly and Unspiritual JAMES 3:15

Any wisdom which might be attributed to him would (like the fire which sets the tongue on fire by hell in vs. 6) be from the lower regions.

The phrase **comes down from above** is a descriptive participle. It defines the kind of wisdom a teacher ought to have: it is a coming-down-from-above wisdom; it is a God-given wisdom. Wisdom has already been described as God's gift in answer to prayer (1:5). Jewish thought often personified wisdom (as in the early chapters of Proverbs, where she "cries aloud in the streets") and pictured her as coming from God. But with the **not** James affirms that the wisdom of the factious is in opposition to this heavenly wisdom.

James describes positively the nature of a **wisdom** which produces jealousy and selfishness. First, it is **earthly.** This word is usually used in opposition to what is heavenly and often has the sense of "human" as against something divine. Thus Hermas, a second-century Christian, uses the adjective to describe the human and false prophet as opposed to the divinely commissioned and inspired one (*Mandates* XI.6). Compare Paul's description in Philippians 3:19 and 1 Corinthians 1:20. Thus James means that the wisdom from which jealousy and selfishness come is a product of fallen human, **earthly** sources.

Unspiritual is derived from the word ordinarily translated "soul." It may seem strange that a word derived from it may have a bad meaning, as here. But the word often has a meaning connected with natural life as opposed to the spiritual or supernatural. Thus it might mean the **unspiritual** or "merely human," as in 1 Corinthians 2:14, or the physical man and the physical body, as in 1 Corinthians 15:44. Perhaps "carnal" could often translate the sense as here in James. The phrase has been explained as "man as he is as a result of Adam."

Devilish should be "demonic" or "demoniacal," as the word is connected with the word "demon" and not "devil." Demons are evil spirits in the service of Satan. In 1 Timothy 4:1 false doctrines are ascribed to the influence of demons. They may influence others to be the instruments of the spread of heresy, but this is the real work of demons or of

JAMES 3:16, 17 — *Disorder*

¹⁶**For where jealousy and selfish ambition exist, there will be disorder and every vile practice. ¹⁷But the wisdom from above is first pure, then peaceable, gentle, open to reason, full of mercy and good fruits, without uncertainty or insincerity.**

---

such as they are. So it is the work of demons to spread jealousy and selfish ambition and every vile deed. Those who possess these in their hearts are acting, at least, as demons do. The wisdom which begets this action is then demonic.

[16] **Jealousy and selfish ambition,** which have already been mentioned as being in the hearts of the false teachers, produce their natural fruits of **disorder** and **vile practice.** This is the proof (compare the use of the particle of conclusion **for**) that the wisdom behind these attitudes is earthly, sensual, and demonic; confusion and vileness are the natural fruits of the evil world and the underworld. New Testament instances of the word **disorder** are 1 Corinthians 14:33; 2 Corinthians 6:5; 12:20; Luke 21:9. The passage from Luke refers to political tumults; those from the epistles have to do with church disturbances. Notice the opposition to the word in this passage is "peace."

The word **vile** means evil in its good-for-nothing sense. It is what is opposed to the "good." The antithesis here is with the "full of mercy and good fruits" of the following passage. The basic meaning is "worthless," but it can also have the meaning of "wicked" or "bad," "malignant" (Rom. 9:11; Titus 2:8).

[17] True **wisdom** is now described. It has already been mentioned in verse 15 in a negative way. The **wisdom** which truly becomes a teacher (and any other Christian) proceeds **from above,** being a gift from God (James 1:5). This is, of course, the kind that James recommends, though he is content with definition and leaves the admonition to the reader himself. Notice that **the wisdom from above** has seven characteristics, as does the fruit of the Spirit (Gal. 5:22f.) and as there are seven Christian graces (2 Peter 1:5-9). Perhaps seven is thought of by James as the typical or complete number.

Peace

The prime (**first**) quality (above everything else) of wisdom is purity. Both God (1 John 3:3) and his word (Ps. 12:6) are **pure.** What is **pure** is dedicated to God and hence is holy. Therefore the wisdom from above is chaste and without defilement. True wisdom produces only what is holy and **pure** (not the evil things mentioned in the context). The adjective often has the quality as an ethical term of the "clean" or holy inward moral attitude: Philippians 4:8; 2 Corinthians 11:2; 1 Peter 3:2.

Peaceable is used of orderliness as opposed to confusion (compare 1 Cor. 7:15; 14:33). It means "not given to conflict," "that which is harmonious and unifying" as opposed to the strife and vile deeds of the earthly wisdom. Much is said by Paul (in whose churches there was doctrinal and personal strife) of this harmony and unity. In a striking passage Paul said that peace should "be the umpire" in our lives, like the official judge at the races (Col. 3:15). Paul urged the Ephesians to maintain the unity of the Spirit in the bond of peace (Eph. 4:3). This is connected to, but it is also different from, the full meaning of peace in the New Testament to express the Messianic salvation, that is, peace of mind flowing from a consciousness of peace with God through the forgiveness of sins (cf. Phil. 4:7).

Gentle is another word in Greek which is hard to render into English. It is variously defined as "kindness," "being yielding or forbearing" (1 Tim. 3:3; Titus 3:2; 1 Peter 2:18). The corresponding noun appears in Acts 24:4 (of the governor's graciousness). In 2 Corinthians 10:1 it is the "meekness" or "gentleness" of Christ. It is rendered "forbearance" in Philippians 4:5. The commentators like to mention the phrase coined by Matthew Arnold "sweet reasonableness" in connection with it. It sometimes has the meaning of "yielding" when one does not need to, that is, to inferiors: not insisting on one's rights. Trench illustrates with Matthew 18:23 as an opposite characteristic in the man who was forgiven and was himself implacably harsh. Thus it is seen that the word carries the idea of "reasonableness" and "graciousness," the absence of bad manners and quick temper.

Open to reason ordinarily means "obedient," or "compliant," "openminded," "yielding to entreaty." Its etymology leads back to the meaning "of good (i.e., easy) persuasion." In a teacher, as here, it would be the opposite of dogmatic and unyielding. The teacher must himself be teachable—ready to be taught and guided in turn. It is a poor teacher who does not learn from his pupils. The word is not used elsewhere in the New Testament.

Mercy means "compassion" or "pity" and is generally used in the Bible as a description of a human attribute associated with deeds of charity toward the poor and sick (James 2:13; Luke 10:37). **Good fruits** refers to deeds or acts, the "produce" or "effects" of the Christian religion that are **good** rather than evil. The use of **full of** to express the presence of something in large degree in a person's character is common (cf. Matt. 23:28; Rom. 1:29; Rom. 15:14). James would insist that not only in the disposition to avoid confusion, but also in the practical results of life the teacher must demonstrate true wisdom. His life must be one of moral and spiritual usefulness. It was said that Jesus "went about doing good" (Acts 10:38). If pure and undefiled religion is to do such things as visit orphans and widows in their affliction, it is certainly to be expected that the teachers of that religion excel in demonstrating this fruit in their lives. Compare Paul's advice to Titus, "Show yourself in all respects a model of good deeds" (Titus 2:7). Especially can they use their tongues as productive of good works and acts of mercy, rather than to sow discord. "A tongue controlled by divine grace can be a mighty influence for good."

Without uncertainty means "a lack of discord," then "lack of variance or partiality." Here the word seems to mean "not vacillating," "not acting one way in one circumstance and another in a different one." James is saying that a teacher in his attitudes should be consistent. Paul often charged Timothy and his helpers to do nothing with partiality (1 Tim. 5:21). The leader loses the confidence of his followers if they get the idea that there is no consistency in his words and deeds or in his attitude toward others.

Without insincerity is literally without hypocrisy.

Fruitful Harvest JAMES 3:18

¹⁸And the harvest of righteousness is sown in peace by those who make peace.

---

[18] This is not a part of the description of wisdom. It is an enlargement of the "full of good fruits." That fruit might also be described as **the harvest of righteousness.** The expression is equivalent to "and the fruit, righteousness" or "the fruit is righteousness, which is sown...." For the expression, compare Proverbs 11:30 and Amos 6:12. In Old Testament parallels **harvest of righteousness** is used opposite to "bitterness" (Amos 5:7; Hosea 10:12; Prov. 9:21; Isa. 32:16f.). Thus a righteous life of good deeds or fruits is what is reaped by the one who sows in the right way. **In peace** stresses that the sowing which produces this fruit is done under conditions of peace (not jealousy and ambition leading to disorder and vile practice). Under these conditions alone will the preaching and teaching of God's word grow and develop into a life of righteousness. **Peace** is assumed as the climate necessary for producing **righteousness.**

Note further that **righteousness** here evidently means "good fruits or deeds." It is conduct and action pleasing to God as in Matthew 5:6; 1 John 2:29; 1 Timothy 6:11; 2 Timothy 2:11. Compare the note on 1:20.

The phrase **those who make peace,** as in Ephesians 2:15, means to establish or bring about peace, so to act that peace will result. Compare our word "pacify." See the noun form of the word in Matthew 5:9. James emphasizes that righteousness is produced in the atmosphere of peace and is produced only by those who are peaceable.

WORLDLINESS IN THE CHURCH, 4:1-12

The Source of Wars and Strife, 4:1-10

Chapter 4 begins with a warning against strife and contention. A connection may be seen between this and the last section in the third chapter. Divine wisdom leads to peace and righteousness. But since there is strife and fighting among the readers, what is the source of such? James answers by

JAMES 4:1   *Worldliness*

identifying the source as the lusts and desires which crave worldly satisfaction. Prayers are unanswered or avoided. But friendship with the world means enmity against God, whose Spirit longs for the undivided loyalty of his children and who gives grace to achieve the purpose. A call to repentance and humility is needed to bring the readers back into the favor of God.

This section, while it may not be pleasant to read and contemplate, is one which ought to be studied and taught. Worldliness is one of the continual problems in the church. Christians are in the world, but they are not of the world (John 17:14). God has accepted them as his children or sons. He justifies them and accepts them as though they were as spotless as angels, but he leaves them here in the world. The final transformation into the image of God himself will come when Jesus is seen in the resurrection and his followers become like him. But God expects them to grow gradually into that image by continually purifying themselves while here on earth as they await the hope of the resurrection (read 1 John 3:1-3, where these ideas are set forth). This divine sonship in the heavenly family calls upon the Christian to break the ties which he had as a sinner and alien.

Some critics think that this passage is exceedingly harsh and even unrealistic. It presents, if taken literally, a picture of sin within the scattered church, which is unbelievable to some. Can it be possible that the church would have grown so worldly in such a short time? Some even use this passage to prove that the book was not written to Christians but is a purely Jewish book which some Christian had later worked over to make it into a Christian document. Note especially the sins of war and murder. Is it thinkable that Christians were actually guilty of these sins? It will be seen that it is not necessary to take these as actual fightings in carnal battles. Even if this were so, it would not have to be assumed that all Christians were acting in such ways, though there is evidence that some did walk the low road (e.g., the Corinthians). If it had been written to Jews, one would not assume that they all were guilty of these sins. Others think that, if the literal meaning is insisted on, James may (as in the fifth chapter)

Wars and Fightings — JAMES 4:1

¹What causes wars, and what causes fightings among you? Is it not your passions that are at war in your members?

---

have been writing to the Jews (Christians and non-Christians) who he hoped would read this book and that he had the Jewish political situation in mind.

[1] The meaning of **wars** and **fightings** is crucial here. Does James mean literal **fightings** and **wars**? Some assume that he does, and it seems unrealistic to them that this should be so among Christians. Actually the language does not demand this assumption. Arndt and Gingrich say concerning the word "fightings" that in the literature covered by their lexicon the word is used always in the plural and always of battles carried on without weapons. In other words, the meaning is always figurative. Its other uses in the New Testament bear this out (2 Cor. 7:5; 2 Tim. 2:23; Titus 3:9). The word for **wars** also has a well-established figurative use. Again Arndt and Gingrich assert that since Sophocles' time the word has been used in the figurative sense of quarreling, conflict, or strife. It will be seen that "murdering" in the same context will fit into a figurative interpretation. Some commentators argue that this is taking the easy way out of the difficulty, but it is also true that they may be closing their eyes to the obvious contextual meaning of the language. It is possible, of course, that James means engaging in actual carnal conflict, and this can be explained in the context of the book, but it is more likely that James means internal bickerings and strife, leading to hatred.

By **among you** does James mean Christians (i.e., his readers)? As pointed out, some commentators have doubted the probability of this. In answer it has been supposed that this is addressed not directly to the Christian part of James' readers, but to the larger circle of Jewish people who (James still hopes) respected him enough that they would read his letter. It is well known that such activity as the Zealot revolutionary movement from Galilee was going on. Many Jews were engaging in this, which was a form of robbery, plunder, and murder. James may have had this circle of readers in mind. Obviously in 5:1ff. he is addressing readers outside the church. Perhaps some Christians belonged to these bands of rebel fighters. If so, their fighting spirit may have spread into the churches. In America during our Civil War, many Christians did engage in carnal war even against each other. But it is still better to suppose that if James is speaking to Christians, he speaks in a figurative sense.

Passions is from the word from which we get "hedonite," one who lives for pleasure. The word in a bad sense means "evil desires for gratification of the flesh." Thus here it is a metonomy for lusts. The selfish desires of 3:14 reflect this. They do not reflect the purity connected with the wisdom from above (3:13-17) and so do not have the peace which goes with it. This is not far different from the "desires" or "lusts" which James had identified as the source of sin in temptation in 1:14. These pleasures were the giving away to the desires of the flesh in a selfish, wanton, and lascivious way, though some think that money basically is meant. For the use of the word **passions** in a bad sense elsewhere see Luke 8:14; Titus 3:3; and 2 Peter 2:13. The strife or conflicts were the direct results of such **passions.**

Such **passions** were **at war in** their **members.** Does this mean among the members of the physical body (as in 3:6) or among the members of the church? If the latter, then James means that the different Christians seeking to gratify their passions found other disciples standing in their way. From this, conflict naturally arose. But more likely James means that such passions fight among the members of the individual's body. So in 3:2 the tongue is set over against the whole body (cf. Rom. 7:23). The verb **war** means "to campaign," "to serve in a war as a soldier." **Passions** (or really the lusts, the satisfaction of which brings pleasure) using one part of the body as a base of operations carry on **war** with everyone and everything which might seek to block their gratification. Some part of man's nature may seek to curb and control and keep under other parts, bringing conflict.

James may be still thinking of the strife caused by the teachers (ch. 3). Or beginning with this he may be thinking of the many different ways that Christians might allow their

Desire

²You desire and do not have; so you kill. And you covet*ᵈ* and cannot obtain; so you fight and wage war. You do not have, because you do not ask.

ᵈOr you kill and you covet

---

interests to lead them to strife. Such may have spread from their Jewish background, but enough of such is seen in the church today to prove that James may be speaking realistically of Christians of his day. In verses 11, 12 we see that they were speaking against and judging one another.

[2] The words of this verse are further explanation of why Christians were fighting. **Desire** is another word suggesting lust for gratification of the instincts. It is a verb form of the word "desire" in 1:14. It means "desires" and here "bad desires." When men live merely to satisfy their desires, they never realize their goal. He who lives for the satisfaction of his pleasures and desires will always "have not." The more he gets the more unsatisfied he will be. Sensations lose their pleasantness when indulged in too frequently. The only way they can then be fulfilled is to heighten the kind of attempted satisfaction. If self-control is not exercised, soon there is no satisfaction at all. Indulgence leads to unsatisfaction.

You kill, or "murder." It is hardly likely that James means this literally, though some Christians may have gone so far as to do such a thing. But there is scriptural background for thinking that James means something else. Jesus in Matthew 5:22 had taught that from the Christian point of view hate in the heart is equal to murder. John taught the same thing in 1 John 3:15. In addition, it is possible that the verb may mean no more than the desire to **kill** (a tendential present). Jesus spoke of those who were killing him, when actually they had only wished or attempted to do so (John 10:33). Parallels exist: Deuteronomy 24:6, where it is said that one takes his neighbor's life who takes his mill as a pledge; in the intertestamental book of Sirach (34:21f.) we find: "The bread of the needy is the life of the poor; whoever deprives them of it is a man of blood." That jealousy and envy lead to murder is argued by Clement of Rome (*1 Clement* 4:7-9).

James does not use the ordinary word for **covet**. It has a double meaning of either "be jealous" ("bitter jealousy," James 3:14; Acts 17:5; 1 Cor. 13:4) or "to desire earnestly," "to strive for" (whence "covet") e.g., "earnestly desire the higher gifts" (1 Cor. 12:31). Arndt and Gingrich take "you are jealous" as the correct meaning. Between the idea of desire (covetousness) and jealousy there is not a great deal of difference. Since the manuscripts have no punctuation, there is uncertainty where to begin a new sentence. The different editors have merely rearranged the same ideas. The language of the whole passage is abrupt, broken into sentences that contain verbs with no connectives. This is a style of colloquial speech (but also of orators and comedy). The brevity of the sentences heightens the points of the description. The best solution is to translate "You are jealous" and begin the new sentence with this.

Just as the "anger of man does not work the righteousness of God" (James 1:20), so neither do jealousy, hatred, and lust lead to God's blessing. "In spite of your strong jealousy or desire, your virtual murder, you do not get what you want." The verb **obtain** means "to attain one's goal or purpose" (cf. Rom. 11:7). God answers prayer, but not all prayer, especially not in giving the ungodly the ingredients for selfish gratification.

James uses verbs in the continuous sense, "go on fighting and warring." The verbs represent the same words as in verse 1. He has rounded the thought and returned to the question "What causes wars?" The whole thought is "Since you lust but do not have, you kill and envy (or covet) and still do not succeed, so you go on fighting and warring." All this is because of pleasure seeking in the bodily members.

The failure to have their desired objects related directly to their unsuccessful prayer life. Either they did not pray for what they desired or (vs. 3) they asked amiss. For some, their attitudes and actions were such that they would not pray. Perhaps they realized that their desires were such that their prayers would be a mockery. Hence they went about trying to get what they wanted without prayer, without taking God into their thoughts.

Wrong Prayers　　　　　　　　　　　　　　JAMES 4:3, 4

³You ask and do not receive, because you ask wrongly, to spend it on your passions. ⁴Unfaithful creatures! Do you not know that friendship with the world is enmity with God? Therefore whoever wishes to be a friend of the world makes himself an enemy of God.

---

[3] James had just said that they did not ask. His style has no connectives. He means "Some do not ask and do not receive, while others ask amiss; and so their prayers are not heard." God does not answer all prayer. His rules for prayer must be met. James has already said that a prayer must be in faith (1:6). Further, it must be according to God's will (1 John 5:14). There are other conditions.

The thing that was wrong with the prayers of those who did pray was that their prayers were evil. The word **wrongly** means literally "in an evil manner," that is, with wrong or wicked motives. What those motives were is explained in the next verse. Examples of the meaning of this word are John 18:23 and Acts 23:5. Some prayers are evil or wicked. "If one turns away his ear from hearing the law, even his prayer is an abomination" (Prov. 28:9).

The verb **to spend** often had the connotation of wastefulness (Luke 15:14). **On your passions** represents the area or realm in which the blessings would be spent. Rather than in the family, in the kingdom of God, or even in civic or social causes, the money was desired that it might be spent in the cause of pleasure.

[4] Now that James has stated the problem of worldly strife and war and pinpointed the cause as their living in the realm of pleasure, he begins a rebuke and prescribes the corrections which such a situation demands.

He calls such worldly people in the church **unfaithful creatures**, literally "adulteresses." Here obviously he is not speaking of the sin of fornication or literal adultery, addressing directly the evil women involved in the sin. This is a figurative or ethical use of the term, just as "murder" is in the same context. Some copyists thought the masculine should be added to make those addressed read "Adulterers and adulteresses." This late reading is in the KJV but does not belong. The whole church is the bride. In both the Old and New Testament God's people are pictured as the bride of God or Christ (Isa. 54:5; Hos. 2:19; Jer. 3:14, 20; 2 Cor. 11:2; Rom. 7:1ff.). Unfaithfulness to the husband is adultery (Jer. 3:9; Matt. 12:39; 16:4; Rev. 2:22). In this figurative use, the feminine form is the correct one. For God's people to live in the realm of pleasure, which in turn leads to envy, lust, and fighting, is to betray the relationship of a faithful spouse as a partner in marriage betrays a husband or wife in adultery. In the Old Testament the unfaithfulness was usually idolatry.

How often have the guilty heard these words: "Don't you know better than this?" (cf. Matt. 6:24). James appeals to the training and conscience which instruction in discipleship should have created in his readers. James is trying to rekindle in his readers the correct attitude toward the world (cf. Rom. 6:16; 1 Cor. 3:16).

The world in this context refers to evil, worldly men who are at enmity with God, in sin and lost. In this sense James had used the word in 1:27. **The world** in this sense is in the power of the evil one (1 John 5:19). It is condemned by God (1 Cor. 1:20) because it knows not God (John 17:25). Christians have been called out of it (John 15:19); they must live as dead or crucified to it (Gal. 6:14). The world lives for "the lust of the flesh and the lust of the eyes and the pride of life" and Christians are not to love it (1 John 2:15).

To be "friends" with this world is to incur the enmity of God. **Friendship** here means affection for pleasures as James has described them. Probably he would include friendship with those in the world (1 Cor. 15:33). If Christians assume the proper attitude toward the evil world, it will hate them (John 15:18, 19a; 17:14; 1 John 3:13). A pleasure-loving, covetous, worldly Christian is a contradiction. Demas was in love with this present world and left Paul (2 Tim. 4:10).

The word **enmity** means "hostility or hatred of God." This means that one cannot love God and the world at the same time. To love the world is equal to hating or being hostile to God (1 John 2:15). Jesus said the same thing of God and money (Matt. 6:24). The mind that is set on the flesh is hostile to God" (Rom. 8:7).

Enemy of God — JAMES 4:4, 5

⁵Or do you suppose it is in vain that the scripture says, "He yearns jealously over the spirit which he has made to dwell in us"?

In Greek James says, "Whosoever would wish to be or intends to be." The idea is that the choice is made deliberately, involving the will and mind (cf. 1 Tim. 2:8; 5:14; 6:9; Titus 3:8). Another possible thought that James may be expressing is that some feel that they cannot afford to be at enmity with God, but deep down they could wish that they were. Such a choice or desire is father to the real thing, as God looks upon it, for he knows the heart.

Enemy of God makes clear the abstract "enmity" (same root) of the previous sentence. The verb **makes** means "constitutes himself." See the comment on James 3:6. One who deliberates the way just mentioned thereby establishes himself an **enemy of God.** He has made the choice, and thus he has made himself an enemy. This is why we must love God with all our heart, soul, and mind (Matt. 22:37).

[5] James starts with the same verb he used in 1:26, "If any one thinks (seems)." **In vain** means "emptily" or "to no profit." If one can be friends with both the church and the world, then what God has said in the scriptures is in vain.

The scripture in the singular usually means a single passage of scripture, though there are a few passages where the meaning approximates the collective sense. Passages where the collective sense is considered the correct meaning by Arndt and Gingrich are Acts 8:32; John 7:38, 42; Romans 4:3; 9:17; 10:11; Galatians 4:30; 1 Timothy 5:18; and the present one. If such is the meaning here, then with Lenski we interpret James as meaning merely that, if man can love God and the world together, then what the scriptures as a whole teach is untrue. In this case, the following statement, beginning with "He yearns . . ." is not meant to be taken as a quotation of scripture. This is evidently the way the ASV takes the language, and it is the best solution of this point. If this is not true and it is considered a quotation from scripture, then there is a difficulty, for there is no single passage in the Bible which contains the exact words of James.

With the statement which the RSV takes to be a quotation the real difficulty is reached. Is the **spirit** the human spirit or the Holy Spirit? There is a variant reading of "dwells" for **made to dwell**, but it is not the best-attested reading. The main difficulty is that in Greek the word for **spirit** is a noun which has the same form in the nominative case (subject) and the accusative (direct object). So only the context can guide and it is not conclusive.

Accepting the reading **which he has made to dwell**, we have four possible interpretations.

(1) The (human) spirit which God put in us longs unto the point of envy. (a) If this is a declarative sentence, it is a statement of the perverseness of the human spirit. It longs (for the world) in envy. This would be an observation on the dispositions of the worldly Christians James has been discussing. (b) If it is a question (as the ASV takes it), then James is rejecting that idea. He is saying, "You don't think that God put a spirit in us that lusts or desires to the point of envy, do you?" His point is that the readers were acting as if this were true.

(2) God (taking him as the subject of the verb) yearns for the (human) spirit (that is, for its loyalty and devotion). James would be saying that, whereas the Christians were cool toward God, his feeling is warm toward them with love. This meaning is adopted by the RSV.

(3) God yearns for the (Holy) Spirit which he made to dwell in us to the point of envying for us. The ASV gives this sense in the first alternate reading and cites Jeremiah 3:14 and Hosea 2:19f. as illustrations. But they throw little light on the idea. They speak only of Jehovah's love for his betrothed. They do not explain in what sense or why one member of the Godhead longs for another. To this writer it yields little meaning.

(4) The (Holy) Spirit which God made to dwell in us yearns for us (for our loyalty and devotion to him) to the point of being a jealous or envious Spirit.

The choice is really between (2) and (4) and the substance of teaching in each is not far different. In either case a member of the Godhead is said to yearn or long for man or his

⁶**But he gives more grace; therefore it says, "God opposes the proud, but gives grace to the humble."**

spirit. The teaching of either is an emphasis of the Old Testament idea that God is a jealous God, loving and craving the affection and devotion of his bride. The fourth interpretation is to be preferred because it is more natural to take the verb **made to dwell in us** as referring to the indwelling of the Holy Spirit, a doctrine that is a central part of the teaching of the New Testament (Rom. 8:11; 2 Tim. 1:14; Gal. 4:6; Acts 5:32).

The translators are divided: (1a) NEB; (1b) Phillips, *Living Oracles;* (2) Moffatt, Schonfield; (3) ASV margin, Goodspeed; (4) ASV second margin, Lenski, Confraternity.

[6] The subject is unexpressed. It is either God the Father or the Holy Spirit who **gives more grace,** depending upon which is meant by the one yearning in the previous verse. If we have interpreted correctly that it is the Holy Spirit which yearns for us, then this passage enforces the concept of the indwelling Spirit's word in us. It is he that gives us the grace, the enabling power and strength to accomplish what is desired for us. This, at any rate, is the teaching of Ephesians 3:16, "to be strengthened with might through his Spirit in the inward man." In either case it may be observed that the passage teaches the strengthening power of God's grace in our hearts to accomplish his will if we will but lean on him. The sense of **grace** seems to be God's power enabling us through his Spirit to accomplish his will. This is a powerful appeal to Christians to love and serve God with their whole hearts.

The verb **says** is impersonal in Greek, with no subject. The ASV sees the previous reference to the scripture as supplying the subject. Other authorities think of God as the one referred to as subject, as in James 1:12 ("which he promised").

The quotation from Proverbs 3:34 in the Septuagint is James' proof that the Spirit gives greater grace, for it shows the direct promise of God to supply grace to the humble. James changes the Old Testament "Lord" to **God** by way of

⁷Submit yourselves therefore to God. Resist the devil and he will flee from you.

interpreting it. The ASV reads, "Surely he (Jehovah) scoffeth at the scoffers; but he giveth grace to the lowly." If we are right in interpreting what is affirmed in this context as being spoken of the Holy Spirit, then by his use of the Old Testament passage, James implies the deity of the Holy Spirit. The meaning is that friendship with the world is pride, because it results from the conceit of man who finds the center of life in himself and sees self-gratification as the purpose of existence.

The verb **opposes** equals "arranges himself against." It introduces the figure of warfare taken up by James in the next verse. When one joins forces with the army of Satan ("the world"), then he finds God arraigned against himself. There is no neutrality. "He who is not with me is against me" (Matt. 12:30). In contrast, **the humble** are those who have denied themselves, forsaken the world, and glory only in the cross of Christ. They are the ones who respond to the yearnings of the Spirit. They are God's friends.

[7] Because the Lord resists the proud (making certain that they cannot win the battle), James urges his readers to forsake pride and place or arrange themselves under God's authority. There is a kind of antithesis in the original, where the same root word occurs in the two verbs "God resists" and **submit:** God sets himself against those who do not set themselves under his authority. The verb **submit** is mostly associated with the idea of rank or order (in an army, for example). Thus it means to put one's self in the ranks as a soldier, resigning his will to that of his chief.

To stand in God's rank and **submit** involves aligning one's self against Satan rather than seeking his friendship. To give comfort to the enemy is treason. The devil is the "ruler of the world" (Eph. 2:3; John 14:30). As James has already said, "Friendship with the (devil's) world is enmity with God" (vs. 4). Peter, too, urges Christians to resist the devil's attack steadfastly in faith (1 Peter 5:8, 9). Peter's roaring lion is actually a cowardly beast. This lion is defeated by a steadfast

⁸Draw near to God and he will draw near to you. Cleanse your hands, you sinners, and purify your hearts, you men of double mind.

---

resistance of faith and **will flee** when resisted. But he must not be given advantage.

This is a wonderful promise from God. He will not suffer us to be tempted above that which we are able to bear (1 Cor. 10:13). Christians are kept by the power of God unto a salvation ready to be revealed in the last time (1 Peter 1:5). To the Christian the devil is bound (Matt. 12:29). God is able to keep us from falling (Jude 24f.).

[8] The condition of successful resistance of the devil is walking with God. If we are to do this successfully, we must get right with the Lord and get close to him. **Draw near** is a figurative use of the verb and is associated with spiritual worship or service to God. In the Old Testament it is used of the priestly service, of those who came near to God at the altar or temple to purify themselves and serve (Ex. 19:22; Ezek. 44:13; Lev. 10:3; Isa. 29:13). It is used of the Christian's approach to worship under the new covenant (Heb. 7:19), especially through prayer (Heb. 4:16). Here it is virtually an admonition to worship God sincerely.

Cleanse your hands is based originally on the practice of ceremonial purification which was necessary for the priest before worship (Ex. 30:19-21). Compare the custom in Jesus' day (Mark 7:3). From this arose a figure of moral cleanliness akin to our expression of innocence: "My hands are clean." See Psalms 24:4; 26:6; Isaiah 1:16; and "lifting holy hands" (1 Tim. 2:8). In the last passage the idea is that, since the customary stance for prayer among Jews was to stand and lift up hands to heaven, the only men to be chosen to lead in the prayer were those who could lift up pure or holy hands. They are to be men of character and purity of life. It is the Christian's duty to cleanse himself from all defilement of flesh and spirit (2 Cor. 7:1; 1 John 3:3). In our present passage the emphasis is upon those who have become backsliders. They are admonished to repent and purify themselves and worship the Lord.

⁹Be wretched and mourn and weep. Let your laughter be turned to mourning and your joy to dejection.

Those addressed are undoubtedly Christians (see comment on vs. 1). They are considered **sinners** because their friendship with the world has made them God's enemies. Consider James 5:19, 20, where those who have erred from the truth face death.

The heart must be set right as well as the life. Compare Peter's "having purified your souls by your obedience to the truth" (1 Peter 1:22), of initial obedience to the gospel. Note that in verse 4, one who "would be" or "wishes to be" (a friend of the world) thereby constitutes himself an enemy of God. God knows our hearts or thoughts. We must be sincere, setting our hearts and hope perfectly on him. He knows if we are disloyal in mind.

The word **double mind** is the same word that describes the doubting man in 1:8. Here the double-mindedness is in holding onto the world and the Lord at the same time, or perhaps serving him with the outward appearance (1:26) while his heart is not right.

[9] Be wretched means "to endure sorrow" or "be in distress." The noun in Romans 3:16 means "wretchedness, distress, or trouble," and in the plural in our next chapter (5:1) means "miseries." It seems best to think of mental wretchedness brought about by the realization of their sinful condition. It is plain that James considers their condition serious. Realization of that condition ought to bring a soberness akin to wretchedness.

Jesus warned that those who laugh will **mourn** and **weep** (Luke 6:25), but those who weep now shall laugh (Luke 6:21). He also pronounced a blessing upon those who weep, saying that they shall be comforted (Matt. 5:4). The thought of these passages is contrition over sinful condition. Peter, when he realized that he had sinned, "went out and wept bitterly" (Matt. 26:75). So did the sinful woman (Luke 7:38). When the enormity of sin strikes home, the penitent is sorry for his wrong. This is godly sorrow which works repentance (2 Cor. 7:10). For the idea see 1 Corinthians 5:2. The rich are

Humble Yourselves

¹⁰Humble yourselves before the Lord and he will exalt you.

---

told in 5:1 to weep for the things coming upon them. Felix was alarmed (to the point of terror) when he heard of "future judgment" but he did nothing about it (Acts 24:25). It is better to **mourn** and **weep** in contrition than to weep too late at the judgment.

The **laughter** is the glad sound of their worldly pleasures. The Christian life is not one of frowning; it is to be a happy and rejoicing life. James is describing here the condition of the sinner convicted of sin who realizes his wrongs are still held against him. This realization ought to wipe these outward signs of gaiety and laughter from him. To laugh under such a realization would be indicative of a hard heart and seared conscience.

Joy here is the inward condition of the sinner, as the laughter is the outward. Many grieve that they are laden with a sinful habit; but to take delight in sin is a sign of perversity. The world's joy is therefore a joy of its own, quite different from the Christian's (Heb. 11:25). In Jeremiah the Lord spoke of the voice of mirth and gladness which would cease from the land (16:9).

The term **dejection** means "being downcast." It is the hiding of the face in shame; it is opposed to the proud look (vs. 6). The publican, realizing he was a sinner, "would not even lift up his eyes to heaven" (Luke 18:13).

[10] James is not speaking of humility as a trait of character so much as he is as an act of resignation, of self-humiliation, of bowing to the will of God. The use of the tense (aorist) shows that he means a definite act, a decisive and full self-surrender such as is seen in the prayer and confession of David in Psalm 51. Virtually the same words are found in Luke 14:11; Matthew 23:12; and 1 Peter 5:6.

Judging Brethren, 4:11, 12

This section deals with the matter of speech, as do 1:26 and 3:1ff. But it is hardly a reversion to that theme. The passage is to be connected with the previous one (4:1-10) on worldly strife. James corrects a specific sin growing out of

> **11 Do not speak evil against one another, brethren. He that speaks evil against a brother or judges his brother, speaks evil against the law and judges the law. But if you judge the law, you are not a doer of the law but a judge.**

this strife—evil speech against brethren and judging brethren. When they become proud and pleasure-seeking, they end by criticizing their own brethren and emphasizing their faults. We cannot have a wrong attitude toward our brethren and be right toward God (1 John 4:20f.). A second possibility is that James is addressing another group of brethren who have not engaged in the sins mentioned and who are disposed to criticize sharply those who do. Rebuke of one another is not to be couched in harsh terms as though the one rebuking were God himself (Gal. 6:1; 1 Tim. 5:1).

[11] The command in Greek means "stop speaking evil, or slandering." The habit was already there. The word refers to defamation of character, or slander. See its use elsewhere in 2 Corinthians 12:20 and 1 Peter 2:1. People who do wrong often accuse and slander others to take the spotlight off themselves. Others self-righteously are intolerant and accusing of those who err as though they themselves are immune from mistakes. "Look to yourself, lest you too be tempted" (Gal. 6:1) is an admonition to be remembered.

Slander and judgment go together. The judgment is the condemnation of one brother by another. In Greek there is only one article, indicating that the one doing both things is the same and that, to some extent, the act of slander involves the act of judging. In slandering or running down a brother the critic sits in judgment on another and pronounces the verdict of unworthiness on him. This is a violation also of the teaching of Jesus (Matt. 7:1). There is, of course, a fine line in the New Testament between this and the recognition of sin in the lives of others and proper admonition and rebuke of those who sin. We certainly are not to condone sin or wink at it. But neither are we to act from suspicion or from mere appearance or personal dislike. Our own attitude toward those who have been in error is naturally critical.

One Judge — JAMES 4:11, 12

> ¹²**There is one lawgiver and judge, he who is able to save and to destroy. But who are you that you judge your neighbor?**

The law under consideration is the teaching of the word of God, probably (if any *one* teaching is in mind) Jesus' law of love. We are to love our neighbors as ourselves. Jesus reemphasized this to say that we are to love others as God in Christ has loved us (John 13:34). This is Jesus' unfailing sign of his disciples. It is Jesus' own "new commandment." If one refuses to obey the law and stoops to slander and evil speaking, he is, in a way, condemning the law and saying that it is no good. Thus he is speaking against the law and judging it.

[12] There is only one who is able to legislate and say what should be done. To judge the law as they were doing was to usurp the place of God. A human is treading on dangerous ground when he willfully sets aside God's law and judges that it is not for himself. He is, in a sense, setting himself up as God. Emphasis in the phrase is on the **one.**

The powers of life and death establish God's right as sole **lawgiver and judge.** God created man; he upholds and sustains him (Acts 17:28); through Christ he has provided redemption for man according to his will. Thus in the judgment it is he who will have the say as to who is saved (will enter heaven) or who is to be destroyed (condemned to eternal death). Emphasis here, as elsewhere, on the law and God as sovereign is not intended to picture God as harsh and arbitrary; nor does the emphasis upon "law" intend to picture the gospel as a rigid, strict legal system. James has already said that man is under the "law of liberty" (see on 1:25). But even in a system of grace and faith which grants freedom from the law, the response of faith and love demands a voluntary slavery out of love (Gal. 5:13, 14) to the will of the one loved; it demands the "works" by which faith is perfected (James 2:14ff.).

One might say, "Puny man! Will you pronounce judgment upon your neighbor when you have no power to save or destroy?" Compare again Paul's condemnation of judging in Romans 14:4, 13 with that of Jesus in Matthew 7:1 and Luke 6:37.

Let it be emphasized again that the sin of judging rebuked here has nothing to do with the duty to rebuke sin from the pulpit (Titus 1:13) or in the proper place to rebuke the sinners (1 Tim. 5:20). Brethren may correct one another (James 5:19, 20), but in all cases the rebuke is to be with proper restraint and with introspection (Gal. 6:1; 1 Tim. 5:1). Judging which is completely out of line is that of attacking one's reputation and good name by sitting in judgment on appearances and attributing motives which cannot be known. Too often we *suspect* that people will do things or are guilty of them, and we say why they have done them, when we actually do not know, and we judge them probably because we simply do not like them.

DIRECT ADDRESS TO THE UNBELIEVING RICH, 4:13-5:6

The Presumptuous Use of Time, 4:13-17

James now seems to turn to another subject—the sins of rich Jews. If we are correct in interpreting this section and the first paragraph of chapter 5 as going together, then the two subjects are the sin of presumption in the planning of life and the withholding of wages from poor laborers.

With their involvement in the business and commercial enterprise of the ancient world, the rich seem to have been guilty of planning their activities without thinking of God and his rulership of their lives. Typical of this were the merchants who planned their journeys and profits with no thought that God might say, "This day your soul is required of you." James teaches that life is brief and uncertain and that everything ought to be done with the attitude "if God wills." Since God's revelation had taught the Jews what their life was and showed them what the good life is, James calls their living their lives in this fashion a sin.

With many commentaries verses 13-17 are to be taken with 5:1-6 as an apostrophe, or a section in which the author turns away from his readers to speak directly to a more remote audience. The arguments for this are (1) the idiomatic

Presumption JAMES 4:13

¹³Come now, you who say, "Today or tomorrow we will go into such and such a town and spend a year there and trade and get gain";

"come now" repeated; (2) the absence of "brethren" in the address; (3) only the practices mentioned with no corrective or call to repentance added (as in 4:8). This is not conclusive, but it is stronger than any evidence for separating the two parts of the section and considering 4:13-17 as addressed to Christians.

The style of this section (apostrophe) is somewhat like the Stoic diatribe, in which the preacher debated in the speech with his imaginary opponent. This has been considered by Easton as definitely identifying the author as one familiar with that device of Greek literature and used by him (on the assumption that James the Lord's brother would not be familiar with such devices) as an argument against the genuineness of the letter. The same style, however, was very familiar as a part of the rabbinical literature of the Jews.

[13] Come now (also used in 5:1) is an imperative (command), but it has no sense of actual going (travel). It is a set phrase, an interjection to gain attention, especially to call attention to what one is going to say. It was used in classical Greek from Homer's time. It is somewhat like our "Come, come now," when we appeal to someone. James is saying, "Had not you who are doing what I am about to discuss better take a second look at your action?"

The nominative of address (vocative in Greek) singles out directly those who are to be admonished. Though the admonition is applicable to Christians as well as non-Christians (Christians are probably often guilty of the defect), evidence presented above seems to indicate that those addressed are the rich also addressed in 5:1. There are many passages in the Bible which warn against the presumption which James is about to discuss.

The reading **or** implies an indefinite number of days or amount of time: One will start one day, another on a different day. The point is that any direct planning that does not remember that God holds the future in his hand is wrong.

JAMES 4:13, 14 — *Business Affairs*

¹⁴whereas you do not know about tomorrow. What is your life? For you are a mist that appears for a little time and then vanishes.

The whole thing is indefinite with James. The words he puts into the mouths of the speakers are simply typical or hypothetical words. One might envision merchants with their charts or maps spread out planning their future trips and transactions. **Such and such** a town means "some" town.

"Do not boast about tomorrow, for you do not know what a day may bring forth" (Prov. 27:1). The rich man (Luke 12:19, 20) thought that he had "many years" in which to eat, drink, and be merry. But God said, "This night your soul is required." James knows that the men make their plans without consideration of God. They have their schedule worked out, even to the gain or profit which they will make from their transactions.

The Jewish writer Philo in Egypt (first century A.D.) gives a picture of Jewish merchants and financiers of his day which shows how true James' picture was (*Flaccum* VIII). James does not indicate that there was anything wrong with engaging in business or making plans. But James sees them as leaving God out; compare his "If the Lord wills."

There was much moving and traveling among people in the Roman Empire. The verb **trade** in this verse is from a root word which meant to "travel"; then it came to mean "travel on business" and "to trade." Finally, it came to mean "to scheme or connive," to "cheat in trade," and thus to "exploit." Though the overtone may be there, James is pointing more to the presumption in the use of time than to shady business deals.

[14] James' Greek is more dramatic than the English. He says, "You say . . . you who do not know of the thing of tomorrow! what sort your life!" We know nothing of what shall be one day, not to speak of a year. We know neither what life is nor what it will be. We do not know whether we will be alive or whether we will be able to transact business if we are. Yet those who know so little of tomorrow talk so. Some texts have the plural "the things of tomorrow."

If the Lord Wills JAMES 4:14, 15

¹⁵Instead you ought to say, "If the Lord wills, we shall live and we shall do this or that."

The **What is your life?** is obscure. It may be a question and a separate sentence, or an indirect question and a part of the previous sentence. It also may be a kind of exclamation. This is a situation where the lack of original punctuation leaves us at sea. But however one takes it, the "what sort" used as an adjective with a noun usually has an ironical meaning as in 1 Peter 2:20 ("what credit is it"). So here it is intended to reduce life to nothingness. Note the way this is expanded in the following references to mist. The point is that we have no certainty of life: whether we shall live or not, be in health or ill, have prosperity or poverty. Of course, if the world goes on and we are healthy, etc., man exercises control, and life may be prolonged or shortened. But these are mighty ifs. In the final analysis we have no control or knowledge of life's issues. Yet what grandiose schemes we make!

The word **mist** may mean either fog, breath, or smoke. Any such rendering will preserve the figure. It stands for something seemingly with us which vanishes suddenly and is seen no more. Even a full life is only a moment in eternity. James uses a metaphor instead of a simile (**you are** instead of "you are like"), thus making the comparison more forceful.

[15] The Greek says literally "instead of your saying." The **ought to say** is a paraphrase. This is (in ellipsis) what James means: You say this instead of saying (as you ought) . . .

The Christian ought to realize always that he lives and has his being in God (Acts 17:28). Nothing happens that he does not know (Matt. 10:29). **If the Lord wills** is not, it seems, an Old Testament expression; it occurs several times in the New: Acts 18:21; 21:14; 1 Corinthians 4:19; 16:7; Hebrews 6:3. Many Christians once used the Latin abbreviation D.V. (*Deo Volente*), especially in their letters, to express that what they propose depends on God's will. The attitude is really what counts. The teaching means more than that we merely preface all our statements about the future with words like

JAMES 4:16, 17 *Arrogance*

¹⁶As it is, you boast in your arrogance. All such boasting is evil. ¹⁷Whoever knows what is right to do and fails to do it, for him it is sin.

---

this as a formula. It means that every plan we make should be made with the certainty that it depends upon the will of God. One may do this without use of this formula, while one might use the formula meaninglessly. God knows the meaning and motive behind our words and deeds.

[16] James calls such statements as that in verse 13 **boasting**. Instead of relying on the will of God, they boasted in their **arrogance** or vauntings. The plural (Greek) may be used because James is thinking of the frequency with which it was happening. But more likely it is an idiomatic way, quite common in Greek, of expressing an abstract concept while only incidentally stressing individual occurrence: cf. "coveting" (Mark 7:22); "partiality" (James 2:1); "murder" (Matt. 15:19); "immorality" (1 Cor. 7:2). The word **arrogance** means "boastful pretensions." Thus James shows that the fault at which he is hitting goes deep. These people were proud of their pretensions and boasts, daring God to interfere with their plans. These descriptions indicate attitudes much more serious than simply saying "We are going to do this tomorrow."

It is wrong to boast against God. Of course, not all glorying is wrong. We may glory in the cross of Christ (Gal. 6:14). But **such boasting** as James refers to here, starting in arrogance and leaving God out, is sin.

[17] The connection between this general statement and the context has puzzled many. Some say that it is merely a proverbial statement which James adds as a general truth without any connection with the context. But it is best seen as a conclusion explaining why the boasting in arrogance is an evil or sin.

What is right is literally "to do good." The phrase "knowing to do good" means knowing how to act in a way that is morally excellent (as opposed to the boastful evil of vs. 16). It means the same thing as "knowing how to live right." The man who by knowledge is capable of living a morally

What Is Right JAMES 4:17

acceptable life and who does not do so is sinning. It is **sin** because the knowledge makes it possible for God to reckon it as sin: "If I had not come and spoken to them, they would not have sin; but now they have no excuse for their sin" (John 15:22 and compare Luke 12:47). The knowledge is not necessarily some distinctive knowledge which the Christian has or something which James is now telling them (that is, of the brevity of life). But the general teaching of this section—that life is a mist (vapor) that appears for a little time—is so manifest and universally true to human experience that it is inexplicable for anyone not to recognize it. Of course, if the Christian has not already recognized it, he has James' specific instruction. So Paul taught that failure to live up to the moral good that is written in the human conscience brings one into sin (Rom. 2). The man who knows that God demands of him to live the good life and does not do it is a sinner. God commands all men everywhere to repent (Acts 17:30).

It is worth observing that here James is not speaking merely of the sin of failing to do some good deed. He is speaking of failure to live a morally and spiritually excellent life when one has the knowledge to do so.

The Sin of Shameful Wealth, 5:1-6

James continues his apostrophe, or direct address, of those not Christians and not his immediate readers, with the "come now" as in the section in which the address began (4:13). But he shifts the subject from the arrogant and boastful living of life without God, in the pursuit of wealth, to the unjust and shameful oppression of workers. James foretells the fearful punishment of God for such sin. Wealth as such is not condemned here. James does not oppose rich men indiscriminately. Those who have understood Christianity as being antiwealth and antiproperty have misunderstood it. It is the wrong use of wealth and the acquisition of wealth in the wrong manner which are condemned, along with the envy and desire for wealth as an end. In this chapter, especially, James is speaking of wealth acquired by robbing laborers of their just wages. One of the sins which Paul listed as barring one from being an elder is that of being

Sinful Rich

¹Come now, you rich, weep and howl for the miseries that are coming upon you.

"greedy for gain" (Titus 1:7). The term means obtaining money by an unlawful occupation or getting it in a wrong manner.

As pointed out above, the rich directly in mind are not Christians. They are such as the rich men who were visiting the congregation (2:2) and who dragged them into court and blasphemed the honorable name invoked over them (2:6). They are not the humble rich of 1:10. The section is a warning to any guilty Jew who might chance to read it. Perhaps James thinks that poor Christians might use it as an appeal for justice to their employers. It certainly would be a warning to any Christian who might be tempted to act in the wrong way (just as the preceding admonition in 4:13-17 is). But James' probable purpose was to put such unjust people in the proper perspective before the church. Those who suffer as Christians from the hands of these people are not to envy the rich. They are to commit themselves to God as the avenger of his people (cf. Rom. 12:14-21). They are to see these sinful people for what they are in God's sight: wretched people fattening themselves for a day of slaughter. The Old Testament had many similar passages comforting the poor in their oppression (like Psalm 73) as well as such apostrophes in which condemnation is addressed directly to heathen countries and peoples (like Edom, Assyria, or Tyre). It is quite possible that James, with his reputation for righteousness among the unbelieving Jews, may have hoped to appeal to this audience as potential secondary readers.

[1] Compare Isaiah 14:31 ("O Philistia") and 13:6 ("Wail," [Babylon]) for Old Testament examples of condemnation addressed as an aside to an audience not directly contemplated in the address. James in the manner of an Old Testament prophet feels the injustice of the situation and cries out against the wrong. The section is thus not primarily for the people addressed, but for the effect on his readers.

On the use of **come now,** see on 4:13. The Greek has "the rich" with the article used in a vocative similar to our

Coming Miseries JAMES 5:1, 2

²Your riches have rotted and your garments are moth-eaten.

nominative of address, a not uncommon idiom in Greek. The designation is of a class of people. James is not thinking of every rich man, but of a class in their overall characteristics. Not all rich people committed sins attributed to the class here. But the characteristics of the group as a whole lead Bible writers at times almost to class the rich with the evil and the poor with the good. Most of the members were among the poor; most of Christianity's enemies were from the well-to-do. There was no large middle class as today in our society.

James uses the same word for **weep** as in 4:9, but the meaning is different here. There it was a mourning of repentance and sorrow for sin (addressed to backsliding Christians); here it is bitter denunciation and prediction of the future wrath of God (cf. Rev. 6:16; 18:15). The word **howl** is a touch of vividness; it is a word which reproduces its meaning by its sound (onomatopoeia). It means to "shriek" and is frequently used in the Septuagint (especially in Isaiah) of the howls of those condemned by God (Isa. 16:7; 65:14; Amos 8:3). James means that, if the rich understood their fate, they would literally shriek over the prospect.

The word **miseries** (the word might be translated by "wretchedness, distress, or trouble") is the word in Romans 3:16 in a quotation describing the wicked and the adjective used to describe the mental distress of the unjustified man in Romans 7:24. The participle used as an adjective, **coming upon you**, is always used in the literature of the Bible and early Christians (when referring to what the future holds) of what is distressing or unpleasant (Luke 21:26; cf. Prov. 3:25; Job 2:11). Here the trouble which James sees as coming upon the rich is either their final condemnation at the judgment (cf. vs. 7) or, as others think, the awful punishment and suffering brought upon the nation of the Jews at the destruction of Jerusalem. Perhaps one ought not to omit the thought also that the rich by their sins may bring suffering upon themselves in this life.

[2] Verses 2 and 3 contain the charge that the riches of the wealthy are corrupted and ruined by nonuse. **Your riches**

JAMES 5:2, 3 — *Riches Corrupted*

> ³**Your gold and silver have rusted, and their rust will be evidence against you and will eat your flesh like fire. You have laid up treasure**[e] **for the last days.**
>
> [e] *Or will eat your flesh, since you have stored up fire*

(as though not everybody's is in the same condition) probably shows that James recognizes that a proper use of wealth could be made (as in 1 Tim. 6:17ff.). But the wealth of these people, being tied up in garments, property, and metal coins, is deteriorating from disuse and testifies against its owners. The stewardship of possessions is a clear-cut teaching of the whole Bible. Luke 16:1ff. teaches that our wealth belongs to "another" (that is, to God, cf. vs. 12). We are accountable for its use. The rich man (Luke 16:19ff.) lost his soul because of disuse of money when an opportunity was laid daily at his door. The rich fool of Luke 12 was a fool for not using what his land brought forth other than for feeding his own "soul." Thus one of the sins of these rich is shown by the corruption of their wealth.

Riches is the Greek word for money, but it also has a general sense of wealth of any kind. Since other words for money are mentioned later, this word may refer to wealth which could literally rot or decay, such as fruits, oils, trees, or vines. Like the rich fool, these treasured up the produce of their lands, but the fruit had not been preserved. In not using it, the owners had lost it.

In eastern countries, and even among the Romans, acquiring expensive cloth (e.g., "purple and fine linen") was a common means of holding wealth (cf. Gen. 45:22; Joshua 7:21; Judges 14:12; 2 Kings 5:5, 22; Acts 20:33; Matt. 7:19; 1 Maccabees 11:24). James had described the rich man entering the assembly as dressed in a fine way (2:2). For the word **moth-eaten,** compare Job 13:28. James' tenses for the verbs **rotted** and **moth-eaten** indicate that these conditions were not new ones. The deterioration had been going on and was still going on.

[3] Another means of accumulating wealth was metal coins which were in use from early antiquity. These they had kept until they **rusted.** The verb may mean "tarnished" or

Fire JAMES 5:3

"corroded." The Letter of Jeremiah (a Jewish document) uses this word to describe the rotting of the purple cloth with which the idols were clothed. **Gold and silver** do not rust, but they may corrode.

The Greek is literally "to be for" something, which means "to be inclined toward some end" or "to be useful" or "to serve for some purpose." There is a difference of opinion as to how to translate the **against you.** Some would understand the meaning "it testifies to you," as if the rich should themselves learn their error from the condition of their possessions. It is better to take it as a dative of disadvantage as in Matthew 23:31 and translate **against.** The witness is about the nonuse of the materials; the **rust** becomes the proof of their sin.

Rust will eat the flesh of the rich. The influence of the rust is transferred by a figure to the rust itself. It will cause the well-fed bodies of the rich to be destroyed **like fire** devours. Old Testament passages emphasizing God's judgments often liken them to **fire:** Psalm 21:10; Isaiah 10:16; 30:27; Ezekiel 15:7; Amos 5:6.

There is another arrangement possible for the words of this and the following sentence, though the sense is not materially different. It is possible in Greek that James meant his words to be read "Their rust . . . will eat your flesh because you have treasured up fire which shall be in the last days." This has the advantage of defining the fire which is meant as the fire of Gehenna. This makes the Greek of this passage agree (literally "treasures up fire") with Proverbs 16:27. It also makes the verb "treasure up" more understandable; otherwise it has no object. It is not usually used as an intransitive verb. This commends itself to this writer. (See the RSV footnote.)

If the translation stands as in the RSV text, the destruction may refer to either the death of the rich Jews in the Roman wars or in the future Gehenna of fire (Matt. 5:22, 29, 30; 10:28; James 3:6). In either case it is a striking way to put it. The rust of unused wealth testifying against them will bring the rich to destruction. Verse 1 has already indicated that miseries are coming upon them.

JAMES 5:3, 4 — *Use of Wealth*

⁴Behold, the wages of the laborers who mowed your fields, which you kept back by fraud, cry out; and the cries of the harvesters have reached the ears of the Lord of hosts.

There is an awful warning in this to the church. Many Christians are blessed with much of this world's goods. We must give account to God for all of it (Luke 16:9-12). There are many things that a Christian may use his money for: for his family (1 Tim 5:4), for his own needs and helping others (Eph. 4:28), for payment of taxes and good deeds (Rom. 13:1ff.; Titus 3:1, 14). We are stewards of it all (Luke 16:12). This is a serious matter for members of prosperous churches.

It is not necessarily wrong to possess and accumulate wealth (i.e., to build an estate). But God's word certainly teaches that it imposes heavy responsibilities and dangers upon those who do. To amass wealth through covetousness or greed is idolatry (Col. 3:5). There is great gain in godliness with contentment (1 Tim. 6:6). With the proper exercise of stewardship money can be used to further the kingdom of God. Many Christians with means do this. Yet many die and leave their estates unused and let them go to the state in taxes or to relatives who are not Christians or are not faithful and who will not use them to God's glory. Many desiring fortunes "have pierced their hearts with many pangs" (1 Tim. 6:10).

If the text of the RSV be followed, then James says that the rich have laid up treasure **for the last days.** This might be the last days of the Jewish dispensation. Or it may be eschatological and signify that James possibly thinks of the coming end of the world as soon. It may refer, as elsewhere (Heb. 1:1), to the Christian dispensation as the last division of time. On the second of these, see comment at the beginning of verses 7-9. James may have identified the consummation of the age with the predicted destruction of Jerusalem and wondered if he was not living near the end of time. This is what Jesus' own disciples did (Matt. 24:3).

If one takes the translation "which shall be in the last days," then it is plain that James means the judgment of fire.

[4] Behold is a Hebraistic type of graphic earnestness. James is intense in his earnestness.

Laborers Cry Out — JAMES 5:4

The word for **laborers** is that used especially of agricultural workers. Palestine was rather unique in that fields were cultivated by hired labor. In most countries the work was done by slaves. James is thinking of the wheat and barley harvests where the grain was cut and shocked by hand. The Gospel references mention **wages** paid to laborers in fields and vineyards (Matt. 20:1ff.). The Old Testament contained special safeguards against withholding wages: Leviticus 19:13; Deuteronomy 24:14. For passages on violation, see Malachi 3:5 and Jeremiah 22:13. The scene here is set in harvest time when the rich would be more affluent and when oppression of the poor would be even less excusable.

James indicates that the **wages** owed the laborers were not paid and that this contributed to the ill-gotten gain of the rich Jews.

Cry out is a figurative use of the demand that injustice be avenged. Quite often this expression occurs in the Old Testament where it has almost a poetic touch: the blood of Abel that speaks or cries from the ground (Heb. 12:24; Gen. 4:10) or the sin of Sodom and Gomorrah (Gen. 18:20). Compare Job 31:38ff.; Revelation 6:10; and Psalm 34:17. Jesus used the figure when he said that if no other testified to him "the very stones would cry out" (Luke 19:40).

The ears of the Lord of hosts is from Isaiah 5:9. The idea of men's cry for justice entering into God's ears is frequent. See further in Psalms 18:6; 34:15. **Lord of hosts** ("Sabaoth," not Sabbath) occurs only here in the New Testament (besides the quotation in Rom. 9:29), but occurs some 282 times in the Old Testament. The original idea was that of God fighting on the side of Israel to vindicate their cause and give them victory in battle (1 Sam. 15:2; Isa. 2:12; 2 Sam. 5:10; Ps. 59:5). But the idea was extended to include the hosts of angels which God might send forth to carry out his will (Joshua 5:14; 2 Kings 6:14ff.). The word thus became one of the highest titles for the power and majesty of God (Isa. 1:24; 6:3). Prayers for help were often expressed to God under this title (1 Sam. 1:11).

The reference here, then, means that the same omnipotent God who fought with Israel and whose word even the

JAMES 5:5 — *Luxury*

⁵You have lived on the earth in luxury and in pleasure; you have fattened your hearts in a day of slaughter.

hosts of angels carried out in heaven has listened and heard the cries of injustice from the robbed laborers. "Vengeance is mine, I will repay says the Lord." All who are tempted to cheat a fellowman should remember.

[5] The wages fraudulently kept back were used to live luxurious and self-indulgent lives, thus adding to the flagrance of their crime. The verb here means "to live a life of ease," to "revel" or "carouse," and carries with it generally a bad sense even in the classics.

The expression **on the earth** is possibly James' way of indicating that this condition is temporary. Only **on earth** (and not for long here) will this indulgent use of ill-gotten gain last. We will take with us neither our money (1 Tim. 6:7) nor the pleasures it buys.

Pleasure again has a bad history. It generally signifies a voluptuous and excessively indulgent life. In the Septuagint it occurs of Sodom's "prosperous ease" (Ezek. 16:49). A compound is used in Amos 6:4. In the New Testament it is used elsewhere only in 1 Timothy 5:6. The whole picture of the rich here is one of wasteful, self-indulgent, luxurious living with a hint of lasciviousness and this off money retained by fraud. Their end is now to be told.

The thought is not unlike Jeremiah 12:3, where the wicked are said to have been pulled out like sheep for slaying and prepared for **slaughter** by the Lord (cf. Jer. 25:34; Isa. 34:2, 6; Ezek. 21:15). The difference here is that the rich **have fattened their hearts** for the fatal day. This is as though animals supplied their own food which eventually prepared them for the slaughter. This fattening continued right down to the day of slaughter. This certainly would fit the description of Josephus (*Wars* V, x,424ff.; xiii,550ff.) for the way the rich were killed, often by torture, at the destruction of Jerusalem. More than likely, however, in view of the overall context, James means the fatal destruction at the final judgment, with the idea of **slaughter** occurring because of the figure of animals used. So James means that they are

Righteous Man JAMES 5:6

> ⁶**You have condemned, you have killed the righteous man; he does not resist you.**

fattening themselves right down to their death or to the coming of the Lord.

[6] This is the climax of their sins. The key to the interpretation is the meaning of the term **righteous man**. If this (as in Acts 3:14; 7:52; 22:14; 1 John 2:1) means the Lord Jesus Christ, the picture is that of the rich Jews (Sadducees) in charge of the Sanhedrin which put Jesus to death lest the Romans take the control of the temple and its rich revenue from them (see John 11:48). In this case James sees the same greed and covetousness being extended in the robbery of the poor laborer's wages. If, on the other hand, the expression is used generically (cf. "the unrighteous" in 1 Peter 3:18), then the picture is that of the poor Jew, wronged by his evil, wealthy neighbor and condemned for this small bit of means. **The righteous man** then would mean just any good man who was treated in this way and who did not resist. Here one thinks of Ahab and Jezebel and Naboth's vineyard (1 Kings 21). The rich in 2:6 were said to drag Christians into court. The solution is not easy. The aorists (**you condemned** and **you killed**) point to a single example (though it could be a timeless use of the tense); yet **he does not resist you** (present) sees the reaction as still going on. This writer would lean toward the idea that James is thinking of **the righteous man** in general and not Jesus, though he could have had Jesus in mind as one of the examples. The righteous do **not resist**. Christians have learned to bear condemnation and death with resignation.

ATTITUDE TOWARD MISTREATMENT, 5:7-12

Admonition to Patience, 5:7-11

This section stresses that Christians (in spite of the wrong suffered at the hands of the rich) are to bear their injustices patiently until the Lord comes, just as the farmer plants his seed and waits for the harvest. It also touches on the expectancy of the second coming of Jesus.

⁷Be patient, therefore, brethren, until the coming of the Lord. Behold, the farmer waits for the precious fruit of the earth, being patient over it until it receives the early and the late rain.

---

[7] Brethren are addressed directly because the previous section had had non-Christians mainly in view. Now the Christians are confronted with their own duty to develop the proper attitude toward their persecutors.

This is not the ordinary word translated **be patient.** The verb here means to be "long-tempered" (as opposed to being "quick-tempered"). The meaning is to hold the mind in check rather than give way to wrath or wavering (as in vs. 12). God is described as forbearing (same word) in 2 Peter 3:9; our sins do not provoke him to destroy us.

The word for **coming** used here is *parousia*, which is literally the "presence" of Christ. The word, which has become an English word (Parousia), in secular Greek referred to the presence or arrival of a person, especially of a visit of an important person. The presence of Christ will become manifest when he comes visibly at the end. Then every eye will see him (Rev. 1:7). This is the appearance or manifestation which is called the Parousia of Christ. This is called his second coming (Heb. 9:28) by contrast with the first advent. The *parousia* is a frequent New Testament term for the Lord's coming (Matt. 24:3, 27, 37, 39; 1 Thess. 2:19; 3:13; 4:15; 5:23; 2 Thess. 2:1; 1 Cor. 15:23; 1 John 2:28; 2 Peter 1:16; 3:4). Another New Testament expression for the coming is the epiphany (*epiphaneia*): 2 Thessalonians 2:9; Titus 2:13; 2 Timothy 4:1.

Christians are not to take vengeance for themselves; they are to love their enemies. "Vengeance is mine, I will repay, says the Lord" (Rom. 12:19). Christians are to bear indignities until that coming.

Jesus used the comparison of the end of the world to a harvest (Matt. 13:39f.). A **farmer** does not expect his harvest on the day he plants. He must labor to be entitled to the fruits of the field (2 Tim. 2:6). The **precious fruit** from the land, which sustains life, comes only after waiting for the season.

Be Patient — JAMES 5:7-9

⁸**You also be patient. Establish your hearts, for the coming of the Lord is at hand.** ⁹**Do not grumble, brethren, against one another, that you may not be judged; behold, the Judge is standing at the doors.**

James repeats the verb (**be patient**) of the former sentence in reference to the farmer. The farmer may suffer several disappointments before the harvest. He does not lose his head, even over tares (Matt. 13:29), and root up or plow up the grain. He does not despair that the grain must grow into a shoot and then a stalk, put forth head, and then ripen.

There are two rainy seasons in Palestine, fall and spring. Grain was planted in the fall and matured with the **late rain** of the spring. So must Christians wait.

[8] You also be patient, like the farmer. The evil treatment may provoke, but toughness of mind will enable one to endure the provocation.

Become "stout-hearted" would be a good way to translate the verb **establish**. It means to "confirm," "strengthen," or "fix fast." Compare 1 Thessalonians 3:13. A Christian needs to gird up his mind (1 Peter 1:13). Faintheartedness not only never won fair lady; it does not solve the problems of life. Fixed purpose and stout hearts are necessary.

John the Baptist used the same word **at hand** concerning the kingdom of God (Matt. 3:2). James wrote probably not too long before the destruction of Jerusalem. This was the final event which Jesus had said must transpire before Christians could look for the end. After this there were to be no more signs until the sign of the Son of man was seen in the clouds (Matt. 24:29f.). After that event Christians were told to expect and watch for the coming at any time. This is the late New Testament attitude and the correct one. We still are to live in this mood. Because two thousand years have gone by since the destruction of Jerusalem we are not to say, "My lord delays his coming." The Lord is at hand every day and has been for two thousand years.

[9] Do not grumble means literally not to "sigh" or "groan," as in 2 Corinthians 5:2. With the preposition **against** it means to "groan in complaint." Troubles tend to make the

JAMES 5:9-11 *Examples of Suffering*

> ¹⁰**As an example of suffering and patience, brethren, take the prophets who spoke in the name of the Lord. ¹¹Behold, we call those happy who were steadfast. You have heard of the steadfastness of Job, and you have seen the purpose of the Lord, how the Lord is compassionate and merciful.**

impatient complain against even those closest to them. Paul used a different word to describe Israel in 1 Corinthians 10:10, but the sin is the same. Israelites in the wilderness lost their perseverance and murmured against each other and against God. Disciples of Christ must be patient toward one another as well as toward their persecutors. To groan against brethren is to risk the Lord's condemnation when he comes. He will judge his own as well as the rich oppressors.

The Judge is standing at the doors reflects the very words of Jesus (Mark 13:29 = Matt. 24:33). The judge is Christ, who, just as in his readiness to forgive and receive the erring (Rev. 3:20), so also he stands as judge ready to open the door to see if his servants await his coming. We know the Lord stands at the door ready to enter at any moment. Shall we murmur under these circumstances?

[10] James is still thinking of the readers who are robbed of their wages. Examples are often the best means of teaching. The Old Testament is full of examples of those who bore up under difficulties. "We are not of those who shrink back" (Heb. 10:39). **Example of suffering and patience** is "patience in suffering." **Suffering** is the Greek word for "misfortune." Compare 2 Timothy 2:9. The keeping back of their wages is such a misfortune. But the prophets also had suffered wrongs and persevered in their midst without complaint (Heb. 11:33ff.; 2 Chron. 36:16; 1 Thess. 2:15; Matt. 23:29-37).

[11] James has himself called **those happy who were steadfast** (1:12). In Daniel 12:12 (Septuagint) we have "blessed is he who waits." Paul had described the purpose of the reading of the Old Testament Scriptures as "that by steadfastness and by the encouragement of the scriptures we might have hope" (Rom. 15:4).

His readers had **heard of Job** in the reading of the scriptures in the synagogues, but the word is not to be restricted to this. Every child was taught the history of Israel from childhood.

Job is the outstanding example of **steadfastness** and was well known for this virtue. The Jews were a suffering people from ancient times, and the example of Job loomed large in their memory and discipline. Both in the Old Testament (Ezek. 14:14, 20) and in Jewish literature his patience is extolled. James includes him and Elijah along with Abraham and Rahab as examples in his book (2:21, 25).

Job's experience shows the purpose of the Lord. The Lord blessed him more at the end of his life than prior to his trials.

The **how** is explanatory of what the **purpose** is: we see the demonstration that **the Lord is compassionate and merciful.** The outcome of double restitution to Job proves the mercy and pity of God. James means to assure the readers that the Lord is no less so toward them, if they will bear their troubles with patience as Job did.

Swearing Forbidden, 5:12

This verse is probably best interpreted as a continuation of the admonition on how to act in adversity, such as abuse by the rich in withholding wages. James had counseled patience and against murmuring. He now in a special way urges that the disciples of the Lord must not allow themselves to be provoked into swearing.

James here does not have in mind what we call profanity or taking God's name in vain. He is thinking of oaths, that is, confirming a statement or promise by something sacred or holy or (on the other hand) imprecations (the calling down of curses on one's enemies in the name of God or something sacred). The use of the verb "to swear" and the syntax of the Greek (accusative of oaths) make this plain.

It is also the contention of this writer that the passage, based as it is on Jesus' teaching in the Sermon on the Mount (Matt. 5:33-37) and subject to the same interpretation, has nothing to do with solemn and serious civil and religious oaths or vows. These conclusions will be set forth in the exposition following.

JAMES 5:12 — Swearing

¹²But above all, my brethren, do not swear, either by heaven or by earth or with any other oath, but let your yes be yes and your no be no, that you may not fall under condemnation.

---

[12] The preposition (*pro*) here means preference (cf. 1 Peter 4:8), that is, "especially." Thus it is not temporal ("the first thing you must do"), but "the most important thing to be aware of under the circumstances is not to swear." The verb means "stop swearing," since the prohibition is the type forbidding the continuation of something. James knew that the frequent taking of oaths was current among the Jews, as Jesus had himself mentioned (Matt. 23:16-22; 5:33ff.).

Do not swear is almost a word-for-word quotation of Jesus' language in the Sermon on the Mount (Matt. 5:34ff.). James changes the tense of the verb thus making Jesus' prohibition more applicable to the situation ("stop swearing"). He also omits Jesus' "at all" and shortens the things excluded as the standards of oaths (omitting "by Jerusalem" and "by your head"). In the place of these James puts **with any other oath** (on which see below). Since James' passage is most certainly a quotation and repetition of Jesus' words, it must bear the same interpretation.

Either by heaven or by earth repeats Jesus' words in part. The Jews avoided the use of God's name and argued that oaths of this kind (compare the "greater" oaths in Heb. 6:16) were not binding. Jesus taught (as the law had, with certain minor exceptions, Lev. 19:12; Num. 30:2; Deut. 23:21) that all oaths were binding. Earth is the footstool of God's feet; it is thus sacred. Heaven, too, is sacred, for it is God's throne. An oath by such things is as binding as one by God's name.

James then varies the construction. In the former phrases James says, "Swear not by heaven or by earth (using the accusative of oath to express the thing by which one swears). Now he says literally, "Do not swear any other oath" (using a cognate accusative). This means that no other oath of the same kind, swearing "by" any other thing of the same kind, such as "by heaven or earth," is to be taken. The word "other" is the Greek word (*allos*) which usually means

Yes and No   JAMES 5:12

"another of the same kind" (as opposed to *heteros* which means "another of a different kind"; cf. the use of the words in Gal. 1:6, "another, *heteros,* Gospel which is not another, *allos*"). This is important, for it bears on whether James is prohibiting oaths absolutely. James uses the term "any other oath" to shorten his quotation of Jesus, and he means "not by another oath like these." Now Jesus' words, rightly understood, do not forbid oaths absolutely either. He says, "Do not swear at all, either by heaven, earth, Jerusalem, or your head." "Not at all" is not absolute in meaning, but modifies the things distributed in the prohibitions and is equivalent in our language to saying, "Do not swear *by these things* at all." But this does not prohibit oaths taken in God's name. Neither Jesus nor James prohibits solemn religious or civil oaths taken in God's name. This is proved by the fact that Jesus himself took oaths (Matt. 26:63f.; Mark 8:12 in the Greek where the same type of construction is found as in the oath in Heb. 6:13,14). Paul did likewise (1 Thess. 5:27, where Paul has the word for "swear" and the accusative of oaths).

Let your yes be yes, and your no be no also repeats the words of Jesus. This is to be taken in context. The Jews took the lesser oaths and claimed that they were not binding. Jesus called this hypocrisy (Matt. 24:16ff.). This made oaths which were binding under the law (which said, "You shall perform to the Lord your oaths") mere profanity. Hence Jesus means that in ordinary speech one should avoid oaths which do not have God's name (whether they are binding or not) and simply give his word, "yes" and "no." This leaves us (as it did Paul and others) free to use oaths in God's name when they are demanded or called for.

To say more than "yes" and "no" by the use of lesser oaths when they are not considered oaths at all is to bring the user into the act of profanity and thus to bring him into judgment or **condemnation.** Jesus had said, "More than this comes from evil." One will be condemned or justified by his words (Matt. 12:36, 37).

The whole range of biblical teaching on oaths is instructive. Moses prescribed that oaths should be by God's name (Deut. 6:13; 10:20). The third commandment did not prohibit oaths; it made sure that they were taken seriously with intention to keep them rather than that God's name be taken lightly. An oath must be kept: "You shall not swear by my name falsely" (Lev. 19:12). "When a man vows a vow to the Lord, or swears an oath to bind himself by a pledge, he shall not break his word; he shall do according to all that proceeds out of his mouth" (Num. 30:2).

The Old Testament used a variety of constructions to express oaths. Some of these bear directly on the New Testament teaching. The most common word for "swear" in Hebrew is *saba'*. It is usually followed by the preposition *be*, "by" (of that by which one swears) and *le*, "to" (to express the person to whom the oath is made). The Septuagint translates usually with *omnumi* (173 times). Several different constructions follow it to express that by which one swears. The most important is the accusative of oaths (Gen. 21:23, "swear by God," *ton theon*).Compare the following variations: "by my hand" (Deut. 32:40); "by the Lord God" (Joshua 9:18f.); "the name of my God" (Prov. 30:9); "as the Lord lives" (Hos. 4:15); "by the God of truth" (Isa. 65:16). This is the standard way in Greek from earliest times to express an oath.

But the verb "swear" does not itself have to be expressed. Frequently asseverative particles such as *ma*, *mēn*, or *nē* accompany the oath, and the negative particle *ou* and the affirmative *nai* are quite typical. Compare Homer's *Iliad*, 1, 86, "For no one by Apollo (*ou ma gar Apollona*) shall lay hands on you." Moses swore by saying, "I call heaven and earth to witness" (Deut. 4:26). Again the preposition *kata* with the genitive is frequent: "By myself" (*kata hemautou*) "I have sworn" (Gen. 22:16). See "by the fear of his father" (Gen. 31:53); "by thyself" (Ex. 32:13); and compare Amos 4:2; Isaiah 62:8; Jeremiah 51:14. The other typical construction is to follow the verb with the simple dative ("by my name," Deut. 6:13 in some mss.; 1 Kings 1:17; Ps. 89:35). In some cases the preposition *en* or *epi*, "by" or "upon," may appear.

The other Septuagint verb is *horkizō*, a causative which means "I make someone swear," or "I adjure someone." It may be followed by *en* (Neh. 13:25) or by *kata* ("made him swear by God," 2 Chron. 36:13). Once the expression "before the Lord" (*enantion*) occurs (Joshua 6:26). Oaths made "before God" or "in the sight of God" are common, as are those made by the use of "as the Lord lives" (1 Sam. 28:10).

The most distinctive form of oath in Hebrew uses the particle *em* ("if") and the emphatic future negative. It is used either with the verb "swear" or by some form of the asseverative particles to indicate the oath form. The full condition appears in Psalm 7:4, 5, "If I have requited my friend with evil . . . let the enemy pursue" (optative of wish). Without the conclusion (but with it understood) this construction was regularly used as an oath: "By myself I have sworn (if) righteousness shall (not) go forth out of my mouth" (Isa. 45:23, Greek). As illustrations of this frequent oath formula see 1 Samuel 28:10; 19:6; 14:39; 2 Samuel 19:7; Psalms 89:3; 95:11; 131[2]:2; Ezekiel 4:14; 14:16; 20:3, 31; 33:27. It is this type of oath which is quoted in Hebrews 6:14 (quoted from Gen. 22:16f. from the Hebrew, not the Septuagint) when the writer said that God swore by himself saying, "Surely I will bless you and multiply you." The Greek is identical with the Old Testament passage in this construction. This is the oath form which is on the lips of Jesus in Mark 8:12, etc.

The New Testament employs the same constructions. *Omnumi* ("I swear," 26 times in the N.T.) is followed by the preposition *en* (Rev. 10:5f.; cf. Matt. 5:34f.; 23:20ff.), by the preposition *kata* (Heb. 6:13, 16). *Horkizo* ("I adjure") and also a compound *enorkizo* occur as in the Old Testament. The usual construction, as in ordinary Greek and the Old Testament, is to follow the verb by the accusative of oaths, as "I adjure you by God" (Mark 5:7); "By the Jesus whom Paul preaches" (Acts 19:13). Paul is definitely using an oath then when he says, "I adjure you by the Lord" (1 Thess. 5:27). This is quite in custom with Paul, who is frequent with strong asseverations in the name of God (2 Cor. 1:23; Rom. 1:9; Phil. 1:8; 2 Tim. 4:1ff.). In 1 Corinthians 15:31 Paul uses one of the particles of oath (*ne*) with the accusative of oaths with the verb *omnumi* in ellipsis: (I swear) "by my pride." Compare also Acts 18:18 for Paul's taking a vow, and see Numbers 6:1-21 for its significance.

Jesus answered in the affirmative ("I am") when he was adjured by the high priest "by the living God" to tell whether he is the Christ (Matt. 26:63). But just as significant is Jesus' typical use of the *ei* with the future emphatic negative (as described above from the Old Testament and Heb. 6:13, 16) when he swore that no sign would be given (Mark 8:12). It is impossible to absolve Jesus and Paul from the use of oaths.

In the light of this, Jesus' teaching in Matthew 5:34 and James' repetition of it in James 5:12 need to be better understood. When Jesus said, "Do not swear at all either by . . . " he should not be understood as forbidding oaths absolutely. It should be noted that "Do not swear at all" is not followed by a period, but by a series of negatives introduced by the particle *mēte* ("neither"). This particle "divides the negative item into its component parts" (Arndt and Gingrich). That is, as Professor J. W. McGarvey pointed out in his *New Testament Commentary on Matthew and Mark* (comment on Matt. 5:34f.), "the universal prohibition . . . is distributed by the specification of these four forms of oaths, and is therefore most strictly interpreted as including only such oaths." Thus the actual words of Jesus forbid only oaths taken "by heaven," "by earth," "by Jerusalem," or "by the head." To take a parallel example, when Jesus said to the apostles, "take nothing with you" (Luke 9:3), he did not give the command absolutely. He followed it as in Matthew 5:34 with a list of specifics all introduced by the same particle *mēte*. Nothing is prohibited except the specifics included in the prohibitions. It is quite obvious even that *one* coat is authorized. In Matthew 5:34 it is significant that oaths bearing God's name are not included in the distributed specifications given. Hence, oaths of this type are not to be thought as prohibited.

What Jesus is condemning in Matthew 23:16 is the type used by the Pharisees when they avoided the name of God and used the lesser oaths so that they would not be bound to keep their oaths. This made these oaths mere profanity.

One might ask, "If Jesus is then reaffirming the Old Testament principles that all oaths must be kept strictly, what is the difference in the teaching of Jesus and that of the men of old which he was contrasting?" The difference is that

Illness

> [13]Is any one among you suffering? Let him pray. Is any cheerful? Let him sing praise.

under the terms of the law an oath "by heaven," etc. (as Moses used in Deut. 4:31), or any other oath not using God's name, would have to be kept or else the swearer brought under charge of profanity or of forswearing himself. But since these oaths lent themselves to profanity in the way they were used in ordinary conversation, Jesus advised against any use of this type of oath. This is equivalent to teaching that all oaths should be avoided except those in solemn vows and in civil and religious situations and that these should be taken in the name of God not in a lesser name.

THE CHRISTIAN IN ILLNESS AND SIN, 5:13-20

Most commentators see the final section of the epistle as a series of admonitions without much, if any, connection or general theme. Most see no connection between this section and the previous one. It seems to this writer that the theme of illness and the issues growing out of it serve as a central idea in the whole section. James begins in verse 13 with the question about suffering. The cheerfulness and singing of praise are simply in contrast to show that one should do naturally what his circumstances lead him to do. From this he turns to a specific kind of suffering—illness—and instructs the ill to call for the elders and let them pray for the sick (vs. 14). In connection with this he mentions the possibility that the sick may be a sinner or backslider and promises forgiveness upon confession of sins, with bodily healing to follow (vss. 15, 16). Then there is the section promising that prayer has power, illustrated by the example of Elijah (vss. 16-18). The last section seems to pick up the thread of the sinner in the previous verses and to encourage the faithful to seek the restitution of the erring one (vss. 19, 20). The whole section is a fitting climax to the previous section on the Christian's attitude in the wrongs he suffers.

Prayer and Singing, 5:13

[13] The **suffering** here is somewhat more general than disease and illness. In its use elsewhere it may refer to suffering hardship, e.g., "wearing fetters" (2 Tim. 2:9) and the hardships of evangelistic life (2 Tim. 2:3; 4:5). James is repeating the same word used in 5:10 when he mentions the "suffering and patience" of the prophets. This verse, then, is a bridge between the difficulties mentioned before (in which the readers are admonished to patience and the forebearing of grumbling and swearing) and the more specific mention of illness, which is the subject beginning with verse 14.

Prayer is the correct answer or solution to trouble. James is not thinking of prayers for vengeance. In James 1:2 the reader is admonished to count trials as joy because they produce steadfastness. Wisdom in such trials is to be sought (1:5) by prayer. In 5:7 they are to be borne with patience. The idea of prayer runs throughout the section (13-20). Prayer is the outpouring of the righteous heart to the father whom it trusts. "God is our refuge, a very present help in trouble" (Ps. 46:1). The faithful are assured that the ears of God are open to their prayer (1 Peter 3:12). "Trust in him at all times, O people; pour out your heart before him; God is a refuge for us" (Ps. 62:8). Jesus taught that God hears our prayers as a loving father who will give his son what is good for him (Matt. 7:9-11). Praying in faith and in resignation to God's will enables us to overcome and stand up under all difficulty and to be better in the end for the trouble (Heb. 12:12, 13). It will also secure for us God's help in trouble; God answers prayer (James 5:16).

James seems to be speaking of general situations, and it is likely that he is speaking particularly of private prayers rather than public ones. He is talking of the Christian's response to his difficulties. The same is true of the following injunction to **sing praise**. In neither case is he thinking of corporate or congregational singing or praying. Of course, when trouble falls upon a group or one member of a group, it is quite in order to call for prayer by the church (Acts 12:12). But James is thinking of what one does when in trouble or conversely when he is happy. In the following verses illness leads to prayer at least semipublic when the elders are called to pray for the sick.

Sing — JAMES 5:13

Cheerful occurs elsewhere in the New Testament only of Paul's efforts to cheer up his companions in the storm on the voyage to Rome (Acts 27:22, 25). The adjective occurs similarly in Acts 27:36. This sentence seems to be put here in contrast to the general subject. It is just as we would say, "Pray when you are in trouble; sing when you are happy." Both are natural attitudes for different circumstances of life. Together they are logical and proper responses to changing moods and circumstances.

A Christian can **sing** even in the midst of adversities (Acts 16:25). But this is because he receives trials with joy knowing that they produce steadfastness (1:2ff.). This is not the ordinary response to trouble. Rather, James thinks that under ordinary conditions singing is the natural expression of cheerfulness.

The Greek word (*psalletō*) is a present imperative ("be singing") of the verb *psallō*. Though James is not thinking primarily of church or congregational singing here, the meaning of the verb is important, since it is the same verb used by Paul in injunctions regarding congregational singing (1 Cor. 14:15 and probably Eph. 5:19 and Col. 3:16).

All uses of *psallō* in the New Testament are absolute uses (intransitive verbs without an object expressed); nothing in the context indicates a meaning other than that of vocal music. A number of considerations have led practically all commentators, lexicographers, and translators to say that in the New Testament the word simply means to *sing praise*: (1) The fact that there was a growing tendency in Greek to use the verb in an intransitive sense with its figurative and metaphorical meaning of "singing" (derived probably from the figurative idea of striking the vocal cords or the "strings" of the heart); (2) the Septuagint usage where the predominant use was of the verb in the absolute to mean "sing," often occurring with words meaning "to sing" in the Hebrew parallel; (3) the strong opposition in the early church (even in the stage where it was still largely a Greek-speaking church) to the use of instrumental or mechanical music. This took such a violent form that it led the Greek commentators to allegorize even the significance of the references to

¹⁴Is any among you sick? Let him call for the elders of the church, and let them pray over him, anointing him with oil in the name of the Lord;

instrumental music in the Old Testament. Whatever the word may have meant at other times, in the New Testament the word simply means "to sing." These are important facts. There is practically unanimous judgment that the primitive church did not use mechanical instruments in its worship.

Illness and the Efficacy of Prayer, 5:14-18

In this section James deals specifically with the condition of illness. The general admonition to seek help by prayer in time of trouble is made more specific in instructions regarding illness or disease. A specific kind of prayer, in a particular circumstance, is ordered for those in sickness. It is worthy of note at the outset that the commentators are sharply divided over whether the anointing, prayer, and healing are (1) the use of ordinary medicinal means with the imploring of divine aid through the leaders of the church as righteous men or (2) the use of the miraculous gift of healing. It is the conclusion of this commentator (though he leans to the second view) that at this stage it is not possible to know definitely which of these positions is correct, since the language and historical circumstances will fit both interpretations. In the comment each position will be examined. The use of the passage both in modern divine healing cults and also in the Roman Catholic practice of extreme unction will be touched on.

[14] The general terms for "suffering" or "trouble" in verses 10 and 13 lead naturally to the more specific words for suffering bodily ailments. **Sick** means to "be without strength" and is used of weakness of various kinds. But the most common meaning is that of illness. The participle used as a substantive is one of the principal words for "the sick person" (e.g., John 5:3). The context makes clear that this is the specific meaning of the word here.

The **church** here seems to be the local church or congregation. In James 2:2 the writer had used the Jewish term "synagogue" to designate the meeting of the congregation. The

Elders of the Church   JAMES 5:14

church was thought of from the universal point of view as an organism, and under this figure it was called "the church" (*ekklesia,* Eph. 1:23; Col. 1:18; Matt. 16:18). But the more common use, and the one more closely related to the history of the word (cf. Acts 19:39), was to designate the local worshiping congregation or community. Thus the local groups of disciples were gathered into autonomous groups, just as the Jews had been in synagogues before them. These local churches had their rulers or managers. Thus we read of the **elders** of the church at Ephesus (Acts 20:17, 28), of the bishops at Philippi (Phil. 1:1), of "elders in every church" (Acts 14:23), and "elders in every town" (Titus 1:5). It is generally conceded from the interchanging of the terms involved in passages like Titus 1:5ff.; Acts 20:17, 28; 1 Peter 5:1ff. that the words "elder," "bishop (overseer)," and "pastor" were not different, but were interchangeable designations. It was the **elders** of these churches that James says should be called for in the case of sickness.

In the modern confusion of church government it is useful to inquire further about these **elders** and who they were. The term "elder" was obviously taken over from the Jewish synagogues, where the elder was a local member of the community. He was not a rabbi or a member of any professional group. Nor are elders of churches in the New Testament ever conceived of as ministers or preachers. They were "pastors" because they cared for the flock, but they did not serve at all in the sense of a local evangelist or preacher. They were chosen from the congregation for their high moral reputation, their leadership, and their loyalty to the teaching of Christ. See 1 Timothy 3:1ff. and Titus 1:6ff., where their qualifications are listed.

Despite the brilliant effort of the great Anglican scholar J.B. Lightfoot in his excursus on the ministry in his commentary on Philippians (later published separately with additions) and those who have followed in his thinking, the monarchical bishopric, which developed in the early centuries of the church (where elder and bishop were distinguished and where there was only one bishop to a church or to a number of churches), cannot be regarded as a scriptural form of church government. It developed too late and arose out of the desire to build up a governing body for the church to counteract the threat of Gnosticism. Lightfoot saw the germ for it in the figure of James in the Jerusalem church and in the evangelistic helpers of the apostle Paul such as Timothy and Titus. Though these may have served as the analogy for the development of the reigning bishop, there was no scriptural sanction for their doing so. Furthermore, though Lightfoot contends that the system developed in areas of residence of the last apostles of Christ to die, there is no proof that they gave their sanction to the system. How early the system actually gained a foothold is tied up in the difficult question of whether the Ignatian epistles present an already settled state of bishop rule or whether Ignatius was merely trying to foster such upon the churches. Lightfoot concedes that, if his argument is sound, there is no escape from the position that history sanctions the logical development of the system into the Pope. His only counter to this is that the Pope should not be a bad Pope! We reject the contention that there is authoritative sanction in the history of the church. In this way every innovation which has crept into the church can gain sanction.

Not the historic episcopacy, but a presbytery, is the form of government grounded upon the New Testament. Yet this presbytery is not that of an eldership over a whole city or region of congregations, but a group of elders ruling each local church. This is the only conclusion which will fit all the data given in the New Testament (e.g., Acts 14:23). What is seen is that a group of men from among the congregation itself was chosen and appointed to lead and oversee the work of the church and to watch in behalf of the souls of the saints (Heb. 13:17; 1 Thess. 5:12; and compare 1 Tim. 3:5; 5:17; Acts 11:30; 15:2).

With this understanding of the **elders** in the New Testament it can be seen that those called to pray for the sick were not what today would be called the preachers or ministers of the word of God.

Let the elders **pray over him.** Is this an example of ordinary prayer for recovery through natural means as David

Pray over Him

prayed for the recovery of his baby (2 Sam. 12), a prayer in which Christians prayed for something to happen in the providence of God (such as the prayer for Peter's deliverance from prison, Acts 12:12), or is this prayer in connection with miraculous healing (such as Jesus prayed before the raising of Lazarus, John 11:41, or as Peter prayed at Dorcas' bed, Acts 9:40)? This depends upon a number of other factors in the interpretation of the passage before us. Certainty about the answer is probably not possible now.

Whether it is the concern of this passage or not, prayers for natural recovery in God's providence or for help and aid in other ways are scriptural. Paul prayed for recovery from his affliction (2 Cor. 12:7-11); and, though he did not receive the answer in his way, he was strengthened to bear his trouble. The church made prayer for Peter (Acts 12:12). Hezekiah prayed to recover and God heard his prayer (2 Kings 20). Paul implies that he had prayed for Epaphroditus in his illness and that God had had mercy on both Paul and him so that he recovered (Phil. 2:25-27). Such prayers ought to be prayed with the attitude of "God's will be done." It goes without saying (in spite of the contention of some "Divine Healers") that such prayers ought to be accompanied with the help of medical knowledge and treatment.

The anointing was to be done **in the name of the Lord.** This means that at the time of the anointing the name of Jesus was to be pronounced, asserting that the anointing was done in that name. Thus Peter said to the lame man (Acts 3:6), "In the name of Jesus Christ of Nazareth, walk." This is certainly the meaning if the anointing is miraculous. If otherwise, the use of medicine in Jesus' name would probably signify that it is to be used with a prayer in the name of Jesus that it might be effective.

There were two common uses of **anointing with oil** which are pertinent to this passage. One was medicinal. The bodies of the sick were rubbed with olive oil (sometimes with that mixed with other ingredients). Instances of this are to be seen in the good Samaritan's action (Luke 10:34) and Isaiah 1:6 and Jeremiah 8:22; 46:11 (cf. Josephus, *Wars* I, xxxiii, 657; *Antiquities* XVII,vi, 172; Pliny, *Natural History* 31:47). Thus whatever is the decision about the kind of healing involved here, the use of medicine in healing is approved in the Bible. Paul approved a medicinal use of a type of wine for Timothy's stomach and his frequent ailments (1 Tim. 5:23).

Another use of oil in anointing was ceremonial. It was often used in the ritual of appointment (1 Sam. 16:13) and seemingly in cases of miraculous healing. When Jesus sent the disciples out to heal by his authority, oil was to be used: "And they cast out many demons, and anointed with oil many that were sick, and healed them" (Mark 6:13). This was similar to the laying on of hands in cases of healing (Mark 1:41) or to covering the blind man's eyes with clay (John 9:6). All these were evidently symbolic, calling attention to the miracle and to the one doing it. Some of them were approved as having effect in healing (e.g., the covering with clay). But as ordinary means of healing such things were not able to account for the results which were produced by the miracle which accompanied their use. Thus the activity called attention to the power of the miracle and of the one healing.

As in the case of the prayer mentioned above, it is impossible to say with certainty which of the uses of anointing James had in mind. Certainly in the context of their own activity at the time, the first readers of James knew which he meant. But that context is not known to us today. We can only say which is more probable and what the application for us would be in either case.

It seems to this writer that the healing was miraculous. We know that spiritual gifts (1 Cor. 12:1ff., esp. vs. 9) were bestowed upon the early church as a means of confirming the gospel in the infant state of the church (Mark 16:20; Acts 8:7, 13). This was somewhat equal to the power of Jesus manifested to heal while on earth (John 14:12), which became one of the signs that he was sent from the Father, and yet which was often used in compassion upon the afflicted.

If the healing which James has in mind is miraculous, the oil was ceremonial; prayer was a part of the preparation both of the miracle worker and the onlookers (Matt. 17:21; John 11:41f.). The reason for the elders' being called is not so apparent. But it is probably because (since the gifts were distributed by the laying on of the apostles' hands, Acts 8:17f.; 19:6) when these gifts were imparted, the elders would be the most likely to be selected to receive them. If this is the correct interpretation of the instruction of James, then the passage has no direct bearing on the practice of the church today. It is obvious both from practice and from the teaching of the scripture that such miraculous gifts did not outlast the apostolic age of the church. Notice the following: (1) The reason for the gifts, the confirmation of the word (Mark 16:20; Heb. 2:3, 4; Acts 14:3), no longer obtains, since the word is fully given and confirmed. (2) The scriptures themselves teach that the gifts were to cease (1 Cor. 13:8). (3) The means of the gifts being conferred (the laying on of the apostles' hands) argues for their discontinuance. (4) Church history confirms this conclusion, for efforts to revive such gifts in the post-apostolic church (e.g., the Montanists) were considered heresies. (5) Modern practice confirms it, because the "healings" performed in the cult services today are never the kind that remove doubt, such as restored limbs, sight recovered of those born blind, or the raising of the dead.

However, if the healing was medicinal and providential, then the anointing served to carry out the healing, prayer was a plea for God's providential help, and the reason for calling for the elders was that such men were leaders and men of holy reputation (1 Tim. 3:7) and their prayers would be valuable as righteous men (vs. 16).

Since it is clearly demonstrated from the New Testament that such miraculous aid existed in the church of that age and since this healing would be more certain to offer aid to the sick, it would seem that it might be expected that the instruction of James concerns the miraculous healings. It is the "prayer of faith" (not the anointing) in verse 15 which promises the healing. The expression **in the name of the Lord** would seem to be more understandable by this interpretation. This passage cannot be appealed to by the sects which teach modern divine healing, unless they can prove that these miraculous gifts were to continue beyond the apostolic age.

The Roman Catholic church appeals to James 5:14 to support the doctrine of extreme unction. In this doctrine the

JAMES 5:14, 15 — *Prayer of Faith*

¹⁵and the prayer of faith will save the sick man, and the Lord will raise him up; and if he has committed sins, he will be forgiven.

---

anointing is considered a sacrament conveying spiritual grace (assuring pardon of unforgiven sins) to the sick in danger of death. The holy oil is applied by a priest to the organs of sense and accompanied by a recital of prayers.

Through the years the practice of anointing with a view to recovery of the sick (as it continued in the Eastern Church) was lost as the anointing began to be associated with the giving of the *Viaticum,* the sacrament providing for the final journey to the soul. In the Council of Florence (A.D. 1438) and then in the Council of Trent (A.D. 1551) it was directed that the anointing should take place only where recovery is not to be looked for. From this the anointing is called "extreme unction," and it is regarded as a sacrament conveying grace and forgiveness of sins to the departing soul.

The Council of Trent declared that such a doctrine was "implied by Mark, and commended and promulgated by James the apostle and brother of the Lord." But many Roman Catholic commentators themselves have said that James 5:14 does not refer to such a practice. The Roman Catholic position is seen to be in error in two specific points. First, the identification of the **elders** with the Catholic priests is erroneous. Second, the changed purpose shows how completely lacking are James' words from supporting the practice. James' anointing envisioned and promised recovery from bodily ailments as its purpose, while the substitute is used only when death is seen as sure and for the purpose of giving spiritual grace.

[15] The **faith** is probably that of both the one calling for the elders and those praying, but especially of the elders, as they are the ones doing the praying. James has taught that when we pray we must believe that our **prayer** will be answered (1:6). Jesus told the disciples that they failed to heal because of a lack of faith (Matt. 17:20). Whatever prayer is prayed, it must be with trust that God can and will, in accordance with his will and our good, give us what we ask for.

Will Save Him

The qualification of faith on the part of the one being healed does not mean that a miracle could not be performed if the one being healed had no faith. This excuse is often seized upon by the modern faith healer to excuse his failure. Jesus would not cast pearls before swine, and he often would do no mighty work in a region of unbelief. But then again both Jesus and the disciples often worked miracles where no faith was involved, such as Peter's healing the lame man (Acts 3). That man was ignorant of what was about to take place; he looked expecting to receive alms. The man born blind did not even know who Jesus was "that [he] might believe" (John 9:36). Jesus raised the dead, as did Peter (Acts 9:36ff.).

Save here means "heal" and ought to be so translated. Forgiveness of sins is mentioned later. This is a frequent meaning of the verb (Mark 5:34; Luke 8:48; Acts 14:9). James promises that prayer will cause the sick one who has been anointed to be healed. The word for **sick** here means "wasted away, or ill"; it is from an earlier usage that signified "fatigued." The word here argues strongly that James has in mind physical or bodily sickness and not spiritual illness as some claim.

Is the promise of healing invariable? God's promises are always conditional. Even in the age of miracles many in the church were not healed. Paul was not (2 Cor. 12:7), nor was Trophimus (2 Tim. 4:20); Timothy, Paul's helper, was to take medicine for his bodily ailments. Those who claim that the gift of healing is an integral part of the atonement of Christ and a part of the gospel to be preached to all must overlook such passages, as well as the fact that the original purpose of such miracles was as a "sign for unbelievers." One condition is mentioned in the next verse—the removal of sin.

Lord refers to Jesus Christ, the one in whose name the anointing is done. The raising is from the sick bed, the effect of the cure just mentioned. Spiritual healing or forgiveness is introduced in the next clause and is conditional. Hence it is wrong to think of the "raising" here as the resurrection.

The condition is one of possibility or probability. This construction is often used in expressing conditions which may not be known to be true or false, but which are known to

JAMES 5:15, 16 — Confess

> **16** Therefore confess your sins to one another, and pray for one another, that you may be healed. The prayer of a righteous man has great power in its effects.

be possible. The perfect tense is used for the present state which is the result of past action; hence, here it is implied that the ill member may also be a backslider or one who has sins which he has not corrected. James is not taking the stance of the many Jews who taught that all sickness is caused by sin. Jesus had refuted this contention that calamity is the penalty for sin (Luke 13:1ff.; John 9:1-3). It is doubtless true that this belief colored Jewish thinking, and it is recognized even in our modern society that some disease is the result of sinful living, either directly or indirectly. But even this need not be what James had in mind. Sickness will often make men who are sinful more conscious of their spiritual condition. Illness has been the turning point of many lives. Thus if the one calling for the elders turns out to be a sinner, he should be helped to realize that to confess his sins and remove them is a condition of his being healed. It is a quite natural thing in almost all prayers for bodily strength to consider the mental and spiritual condition of the patient and to ask forgiveness and spiritual strengthening at the same time.

The verb **forgiven** is impersonal: "It shall be remitted for him." The same sort of impersonal construction occurs in Matthew 12:32. This forgiveness is conditional as always. The condition is the subject of the next clause—confession.

[16] The **therefore** does not occur in all manuscripts, but it is almost certainly genuine. This is important, as it serves to connect the thought. The sense is: "For this reason confess your sins." If the sick man is a sinner, he may be forgiven; and to achieve this, the condition of forgiveness (which is confession and which presumes repentance) is enjoined. The principle of mutual confession of sins is wider than the primary context of this passage (1 John 1:7f.); nevertheless this is the specific application of the reference. The verse is connected with the forgiveness of the sick, with whom the whole section is concerned. The word **confess** refers to an open admission of a fact—here a wrongdoing. John the Baptist "confessed, he did not deny" (John 1:20). James uses a present imperative of continuous action: "Be in the practice of confessing your sins to one another." We are not to wait until we are ill to do so.

Not merely "faults" (as in the KJV) but **sins** are to be confessed. James repeats the same word of the previous verse, "if he has committed sins."

To one another does not refer to confession to a person of sins committed against him; though, if one is guilty of such, they ought to be confessed and made right. But James is thinking of unburdening our lives to each other (and here to the elders in particular) at such time as this, in order that we may intercede for one another.

In view of the general nature of the rule as stated, it should be emphasized that the verse does not limit the confession to the elders. Any brother may be of help to another in bearing the burden of his trespass (Gal. 6:1). This may, as is often done, be before the whole church. In fact, if the sin is of such a nature that the whole church is affected, the confession should be before the congregation. But the principle is much more general than this.

The Roman Catholic doctrine of auricular confession has no support from this passage. In the first place, "elders" here does not refer to a priestly set of workers. Elders here are not given power to absolve a sinner or to set conditions on which he may be forgiven. The only conditions of forgiveness are those laid down in the gospel of confession and repentance (which implies restitution)—Acts 8:22; 1 John 1:7-9. The confession is for intercession and then for healing and is not for absolution. Finally, **to one another** means that any brother chosen may rightly hear the confession and make intercession.

Pray "in behalf of one another" as well as **confess to one another.** Simon asked Peter to pray for him that he not perish with his money (Acts 8:24).

That you may be healed returns to the main subject of bodily healing. For the one who is ill and also in sin, the sin stands between him and being healed. If he is willing to confess his sin and seek forgiveness, the elders may pray for him as they were called to do. The anointing and praying would then be in order. Verse 15 promised that the prayer would be effective.

The noun **prayer** means "entreaty." It is petition, the begging or imploring of God for what one desires. It is generally used of prayer, but of a particular kind of prayer—an earnest entreaty for something for which one longs. It is not necessarily selfish to let God know our wants so long as we are sincere and our desires are not selfish or evil (James 4:3). Here James is encouraging prayer for recovery from sickness and for another's sins. Christians may pray for many things. What is generally worth a Christian's time and efforts surely is worth his prayers.

The **righteous man** in this passage and possibly in verse 6 is the godly or upright man, the one endeavoring to please God in life, though suffering persecution. The word is a virtual synonym of "a Christian" as opposed to those that are evil and disobedient (Matt. 13:41-43, 49; see Matt. 25:32, 46). The two groups are often contrasted in the epistles: 1 Peter 3:12; 4:15; Hebrews 12:23; Revelation 22:11. In 1 Timothy 2:8 the men wh9 can lift holy hands are to pray. Many passages in both Old and New Testaments express the idea that God listens to the man who walks in his ways: Psalm 34:12ff. (quoted in 1 Peter 3:10ff.); Genesis 18:23-32; John 9:31; Proverbs 15:29; 28:9; Psalm 66:18.

Has great power is a very strong expression. The verb means to "have strength," to "be powerful or mighty," and then to "prevail, to win out" (cf. Acts 19:20). Here the meaning is something like "is able to do much." For an illustration James tells what Elijah's prayer did. Compare Romans 3:2.

The verb *energeō* (**in its effects**) as an intransitive verb (as in this passage) means to "work, be at work, operate, be effective." Because the word has caused no little difficulty, it is well to study the other uses of it. In Philippians 2:13 it is used as an infinitive like a noun: "God is at work in you both to will and *to work*." Here the infinitives mean "willingness" and "action." It is used as a finite verb: Matthew 14:2 = Mark 6:14, "(John's) powers *are at work* in him (Christ)"; Romans

Elijah

[17]Elijah was a man of like nature with ourselves and he prayed fervently that it might not rain, and for three years and six months it did not rain on the earth.

7:5, "Passions . . . *were at work* in our members to bear fruit for death"; 2 Corinthians 4:12, "Death *is at work in us*"; 1 Thessalonians 2:13, "(the word) which *is at work* in you believers"; 2 Thessalonians 2:7, "the mystery of lawlessness *is* already *at work.*"

But more in point are the other passages where it is used as a participle with an adjectival or modifying force: Ephesians 2:2, "the prince of the power of the air, the spirit that is now *at work* in the sons of disobedience"; 2 Corinthians 1:6, "Your comfort which you *experience*"; Ephesians 3:20, "by the power *at work* (operative, effective) within us"; Colossians 1:29, "striving with all the energy (*energeian*, a noun) which he mightily inspires (*working*, the participial adjective) within me"; and Galatians 5:6, "faith *working* through love."

In the light of these parallels James means that a prayer which is "working, operative, or doing" is the prayer which is very strong or prevailing with God. Lenski's translation is "A righteous one's petition avails a great deal when putting forth its energy." "Effectual" is thus a proper translation as it keeps the adjectival force; **in its effects**, however, does not do this. The petition of a righteous man avails when it is doing its work, which is petitioning, pleading, begging. The action of prayer must be earnestly and persistently engaged in. God does not want to interpret our own desires and thoughts; he wants us to express them. Prayer is often an unused asset. This is importunity. Consider the cases of the persistent friend (Luke 11:5-8), the importunate widow (Luke 18:1-8), and the imploring Canaanite mother (Matt. 15:21-28). They would not take no for an answer. God is touched when the petitions of a righteous man are going on persistently, when they are doing their work.

[17] The subject of the efficacy of prayer in raising the sick leads to an illustration of the power of prayer: the prayer of **Elijah** began and ended the great drought in Israel in

Ahab's time (1 Kings 17). It has been supposed that James may have turned to Elijah's example by the natural connection between praying for the recovery of the sick and the prophet who raised the son of the widow of Zarephath by prayer (1 Kings 17:17). Even if this is true, he still takes another and perhaps more dramatic illustration of this prophet's prayer life. Elijah's example was well impressed upon the Jewish mind. Jesus mentioned his miracle on the son of the widow and spoke of the same amount of time lapsed in the drought (Luke 4:25).

Of like nature means of similar feeling or sensations. Compare Acts 14:15, where Paul asserts to the people of Lystra that he and Barnabas were men of like passions with them—not gods. Elijah had the same kind of feelings, circumstances and experiences as we. The idea is that basically he was no different from us. If God answered his prayer, why not ours? But why this statement? Because the Jews of the intertestamental period developed an exaggerated opinion of Elijah, making him a mysterious heavenly figure, as they did Enoch and Melchizedek. Peter had to correct Cornelius by telling him that he was also a man (Acts 10:26). Hebrews in much the same way insists that Jesus was "made like his brethren" (2:17). If it is thought that Elijah was some sort of extraordinary figure, then his prayer might be different from ours. The same power of prayer is within the reach of the church, since we are the same kind of creatures that Elijah was.

He prayed fervently is literally "he prayed with prayer." This is a Hebraism. The construction is emphatic, suggesting intensity or earnestness. There are many examples in the New Testament of this mode of thinking and speaking. Compare "desired with desire" (Luke 22:15) and "charge with charging" (Acts 5:28). The RSV has therefore correctly caught the thought in its **fervently.**

There is no mention of this prayer in the Old Testament. Elijah only declared that there would be no dew or rain in Israel except by his word (1 Kings 17:11f.), according to our records. But Jesus implied the same fact about him (Luke 4:25). If it was not to rain except by his word, then he must

18Then he prayed again and the heaven gave rain, and the earth brought forth its fruit.

have consulted God about the fact and have known that his prayer would be answered. If James, then, knew the length of the drought, it would be a simple deduction that Elijah had continued his prayer over this time until God was ready once more to send him to Ahab with the promise of rain.

The Old Testament does not specify the length of time, but that proves nothing. There is nothing in the Old Testament to contradict it. First Kings 18:1 says that in the third year Elijah was told to go show himself to Ahab. But this is the third year from what? The Bible does not say that it was only in the third year of the drought. Nor does Kings say how long it was from then until the drought was broken. So the Old Testament does not prove James wrong.

[18] The story of this prayer and its results is told in detail in the story of the contest on Mt. Carmel (1 Kings 18:20-45). After Elijah began praying, he prayed seven times before the servant reported a small cloud coming up over the sea. After this "the heavens grew black with clouds and wind, and there was a great rain" (1 Kings 18:45).

Did Elijah's prayers which were answered in the withholding and sending of rain result in miracles, and may we expect the same? Is this what James is saying in stressing that Elijah was like us? In a sense, the result was unnatural and miraculous. But it may be noted that, when the rain came, it came in the natural way—through clouds, which had hitherto not arisen. Strictly speaking, the answer was providential (if we are to make a strict distinction). All answers to prayers need not be thought of as miracles. In Bible times God answered some prayers for healing with a miracle—the gift of healing. But the prayer of faith in connection with the physician may help to heal; the modern physicians say so themselves. The prayer of forgiveness in the same context did not require miraculous manifestation. The point of comparison is that, whether prayer is answered in the same way as Elijah's was answered or not, since we are the same kind of creatures, God can and will hear and answer our prayers.

> [19] **My brethren, if any one among you wanders from the truth and some one brings him back,**

Converting Erring Brethren, 5:19, 20

In this final section James is still thinking of praying for the erring brother. In verse 15 he has mentioned the forgiveness of sins which the sick brother may have in his life. The brother's healing will depend upon his confession. But the touching of such a brother and turning him from his way may be a difficult task. James teaches the spiritual what a favor one does another when he is the instrument of leading that brother to be rid of his sins.

[19] Five times in the admonitions of this chapter James addresses his readers affectionately as **brethren.** He is in deep earnest over the lost.

James is thinking of the sinning Christian, as in 5:15, 16. There he used the perfect tense of people who were in a state of sin as a result of past actions. He is thinking of a backslider or of one who may be still attending services, but who is known to be in a dangerous state of fault. Many brethren have quit the church after having been overtaken in a trespass (Gal. 6:1ff.). Serious illness and the admonition and pleading of brethren have often rescued such. To **wander from the truth** is to be deceived and thus led away from the truth, the truth being the gospel of Jesus Christ. It is possible for one to deceive himself or be deceived by others. Those not Christians are often deceived about the truth. But those James is concerned about are deceived and led away from the truth after having received it, i.e., backsliders or apostates. Those commentators who think of the Jewish readers who have been tempted to go back to Judaism may be correct. See Hebrews 2:1ff.; 6:4-8; 10:25ff. But moral as well as doctrinal sins are possible. James' conditional sentences are of real possibilities (compare on vs. 15). One could not wander from the truth unless he had been in it; **the death** from which he will save his soul, if one convert him, must certainly be eternal death.

The word **brings back** means to "turn someone back" in a religious or moral sense. John the Baptist was to turn many to

> **[20]** let him know that whoever brings back a sinner from the error of his way will save his soul from death and will cover a multitude of sins.

the Lord (Luke 1:16). The conversion is "from the error of his way" (next verse). One does this by bringing the sinner to his senses through the word of God by teaching, warning, pleading, admonishing, and showing an interest in him. Though the scriptures teach that some put themselves beyond repentance (Heb. 6:4ff.), there are many who fall away who could be won back to Christ. James may be thinking of the many Jews who, now that the Judaism of their fathers had begun to harden against Christianity, were finding the way difficult. He may remember that he himself had once not believed in the claims of his brother Jesus.

[20] James is anxious to point to the knowledge of the favor that one does in helping the erring. It is difficult for us to realize the value of a soul. This is beyond our understanding. The best way to realize the value of a soul is to remember what it cost to redeem one—the blood of Jesus.

Death here is eternal death, the second death of the Bible. Repentance will not save a man's soul from dying any other death. To die and be lost is a horrible thing to contemplate. To realize that to rescue a brother is to **save his soul** is indeed an important realization. We are our brother's keeper.

Cover a multitude of sins is repetition of a kind. To **cover sins** in the Old Testament sense is to have them forgiven. The passage (like 1 Peter 4:8) is based on Proverbs 10:12. Notice the parallelism in Psalm 85:2 (Greek), "Thou hast forgiven thy people their lawless deeds; thou hast covered all their sins." Nehemiah's prayer for his enemies was "Do not cover their guilt, and let not their sin be blotted out from thy sight" (Neh. 4:5).

There has been some question as to whose sin James is saying will be covered by converting the sinner. Oesterley argues that James is stating the doctrine of the Jews of the merit of balancing an evil deed with a good one and refers it to the one converting the erring. The passage could refer to the one converting the sinner without having this meaning.

Jesus said that, if we forgive others, we will be forgiven. This is not as a matter of merit, but is creating or showing the right attitude on our part, which in turn disposes God to be merciful to us. So James taught that God will show mercy to the merciful (2:13). But on the whole, it is better to take James as thinking of the **multitude of sins** (vs. 15) of the sinner. To convert him is to have these sins removed and to save him from death. This is indeed a labor worthy of a Christian.

James breaks off the letter without any farewell. He had signed the letter at the start as was typical of epistles in those days. He was not writing a personal letter to acquaintances or to a particular church known to him. This fact, together with his style of moving from one subject to another somewhat rapidly, left him with no special need to end with a salutation. The first epistle of John likewise has no formal closing. A few cursive manuscripts of James and one Syrian source add "Amen," but it is not genuine.